FR. PETER MARY ROOKEY

FR. PETER MARY ROOKEY

A LABORER OF THE HARVEST IN THE LORD'S VINEYARD

POLAND, DECEMBER 10-21, 2004

Compiled and Edited by

BARBARA WOJTOWICZ

Library of Congress Control Number: 2007901529
ISBN: Hardcover   978-1-4257-6158-5
               Softcover   978-1-4257-6154-7

Original title: *O. Peter Rookey, OSM, Robotnik Zniwa Panskiego*

Copyright for the Polish publication 2005 by Barbara Wojtowicz
for Piarists Order Publishers, Kraków, Poland

Assistance in collection of the materials: Danuta Felix, Danuta Lis,
Danuta Michalowska, Helena Sosnowska, Urszula Uljasz

Front cover photograph: Br. Hieronim Majka, CSSp
Back cover photograph: courtesy of Timothy Rookey
Interior photographs: Br. Hieronim Majka, CSSp, Fr. John Taff, SP,
and Piotr Wasacz
Cover design: Kelley Witzemann

Translation from Polish to English: Tadeusz Trzaskowski

Copyediting: Barbara Wojtowicz
Linguistic revision: Kathleen Quasey
Consultation: James Hrechko

Computer file processing and saving: Arthur Wojtowicz

This book was printed in the United States of America.

To order additional copies of this book, contact:
Xlibris Corporation
1-888-795-4274
www.Xlibris.com
Orders@Xlibris.com
36263

This book is issued as a humble Act of Thanksgiving to God the Father, the Son, and the Holy Spirit, as well as to Mary, Mother of God and Our Mother for having conferred the Gift of Priesthood upon Father Peter Mary Rookey, OSM, for the sake of us and our times.

ACKNOWLEDGMENTS

This English version of the Polish book about Fr. Peter Mary Rookey's visit to Poland in December 2004 could not have materialized had it not been for the unfailing support of some very special individuals. And those individuals can never be thanked enough; namely: **Kathy Quasey**—for her loyalty, emotional support, and encouragement; **James Hrechko, SOSM**—for his incessant assistance, patience, and spiritual support; and **Irene Silberman, Earl Thomas Rookey, Jozefa Papaj, Patrick Fagan, Stefania Chase, MD, and Paul Byrne**—for their financial support for the English translation that facilitated further processing of this book.

All those dear friends were God-inspired, Angel-like helpers at that particular time, and not only then.

May Our Lord reward them by His unlimited measures of His Generosity.

Fr. Peter Mary Rookey, OSM.

The Miracle Prayer

Lord Jesus, I come before You just as I am.
I am sorry for my sins. I repent of my sins, please forgive me.
In Your name I forgive all others for what they have done against me.
I renounce satan, the evil spirits and all their works.
I give you my entire self, Lord Jesus, now and forever.
I invite you into my life, Jesus. I accept You as my Lord, God, and Savior.
Heal me, change me, strengthen me in body, soul, and spirit.
Come, Lord Jesus, cover me with Your Precious Blood
and fill me with Your Holy Spirit.
I love You, Lord Jesus. I praise You, Jesus. I thank You, Jesus.
I shall follow You every day of my life. Amen.

Mary, my Mother, Queen of Peace; St. Peregrine, the Cancer Saint;
all you Angels and Saints, please help me. Amen.

Imprimatur+ Francisco Maria Aguilera Gonzalez, Auxiliary Bishop of Mexico, September 8, 1992

Say this Prayer faithfully, no matter how you feel, when you come to the point where you sincerely mean each word, with all your heart, something good spiritually will happen to you. You will experience Jesus, and **He** will change your whole life in a very special way. You will see.

CONTENTS

IV. FATHER PETER MARY ROOKEY, OSM, WITH THE PIARIST FATHERS IN WARSZAWA, ŁOWICZ, RZESZÓW, JASŁO, AND KRAKÓW

No one who lights a lamp conceals it with a vessel or sets it under a bed;
rather, he places it on a lamp stand so that those who enter may see the light.

(Lk 8:16)

Editor's Note

Many books would not materialize without the aid and contribution of special people. And those special people were all the participants of meetings with Fr. Peter Mary Rookey held during his visit to Poland in December 2004. It is to all of those participants that we deliver this book—a recording of the experiences, impressions, reflections, deliberations, and, above all, the Divine Graces received and, upon encouragement, contributed by some of those participants for sharing with others.

The original, rather modest, number of 15 contributing persons grew to 55, a number large enough to fit the scope of a single book publication but only a fraction of the estimated 50 000 people whose individual experiences of those memorable 10 days of December 2004 wrought smaller or greater changes in their lives, preserved deeply in their hearts and memories.

For all whom this book will reach, may it be a sign of the eternal, invariably gracious and merciful presence of God among us and an inspiration to lead our lives by incessantly giving thanks to God for all that comes from Him.

Barbara Wojtowicz

Publisher's Note

Issued by the Piarists' Publishing House, the Polish version of the book by H. Parsons, *Man of Miracles,* has stirred a vivid interest among its readership in both the person of Fr. Peter Mary Rookey and the kind of prayer ministry performed by him. In the spring of 2004, Fr. Peter made a short stopover in Kraków, Poland, on his way back from the Holy Land and concelebrated an evening mass at the local Piarist Fathers' church. Although only some of the people were informed just a couple of hours ahead of the time about his brief visit, the faithful filled up the church, which was proof of how they were strongly willing to come to see Fr. Peter in person.

In the early fall of 2004, both the Jesuit Fathers in Bydgoszcz and the Piarist Fathers in Krakow were the initiators of inviting Fr. Peter to Poland officially. Many words of gratitude should go to Fr. Mieczysław Łusiak, SJ, who, with great devotion, provided the accommodation and care for this honorable guest during his stay in Bydgoszcz. On the Piarists' part, the organizational matters were provided by Fr. Stanisław Kania, SP, who played the role of Fr. Peter's personal chauffer, guide, and attendant.

This publication was possible thanks to those who had desired to share their experiences and reflections after meeting with Fr. Peter. We invite those who also would like to describe their experiences to cooperate with our publishing house. Maybe a new book will be developed and, maybe, it will help in extending a new invitation for Fr. Peter to come to Poland again.

Fr. Stanislaw Kania, SP

I

PROLOGUE

THE CURRICULUM VITAE OF
FATHER PETER MARY ROOKEY, OSM

Fr. Peter Mary Rookey, OSM, was born on October 12, 1916, in Superior, Wisconsin. He entered the Servite Seminary in Hillside near Chicago, Illinois, in 1930.

He studied theology, philosophy, and music at two Chicago universities: Loyola and DePaul.

On May 17th, 1941, he was ordained at Our Lady of Sorrows Basilica in Chicago. He spent his first two years of priesthood in Milwaukee, Wisconsin, where he was an assistant to the master of both the Novitiate and the Servites' College. He lived for 4 years in Portland, Oregon, at the National Chapel of the Friar Servants of Our Lady of Sorrows, where he gained experience in running a parish. Next, he spent 1 year at the Servite Seminary in Hillside near Chicago.

In August 1948, he moved to Northern Ireland to assist Fr. James Mary Keane, OSM, in establishing the first Irish foundation of the Servites—Our Lady of Benburb, County Tyrone. He directed the College of Our Lady of Benburb for 3 years. At that time, he became well-known for the effectiveness of his intercessional prayers.

In 1953, he was elected to the office of the Assistant General of the Servite Order with residence in Rome, Italy. Holding that position enabled him to travel widely to Belgium, Ireland, Africa, and the Middle East.

From 1959 to 1961, he directed the International Catholic College at the University of Louvain in Belgium (founded in the 13th century AD). Afterward, there followed 5 years of living in Germany, Sweden, and the Middle East.

In 1968, he returned to the US, where for 16 years he was assigned to four mission churches in the Missouri Ozarks. He then returned to the place of his ordination, the Basilica of Our Lady of Sorrows in Chicago, where he served from 1985 through 1989.

His healing ministry was reinstated in 1986, after a long pause of 33 years.

Currently, his International Compassion Ministry is headquartered in the suburbs of Chicago (Olympia Fields, Illinois). He ministers far and near over the telephone and through letters.

Fr. Peter Mary was featured in many newspaper articles witnessing to God's Power through prayers. He is the author of a book titled *The Shepherd of Souls* on the life of St. Anthony Pucci (also a Servant of Mary). Fr. Peter was honored by the late Pope John Paul II who designated him a Knight of the Holy Sepulchre.

FATHER PETER MARY ROOKEY, OSM: A LABORER OF THE HARVEST IN THE LORD'S VINEYARD

In his office (International Compassion Ministry located in the suburbs of Chicago), Fr. Peter receives phone calls from people of all continents, asking for intercessional prayers. Together with a team of his aides, he patiently and devotedly responds with prayers and love to all such telephone calls, in which requests for prayer for the healing of body, mind, and/or soul are made. The phone lines are bustlingly busy all the time.

The ministry of Fr. Peter Mary Rookey has been beneficial to a countless number of people from all corners of his native land, ie, the United States, and other countries of the world; people who have received all sorts of Divine Graces (confirmed by a great number of testimonies and thank-you letters received). His healing Holy Masses have gathered thousands of people suffering from all kinds of possible diseases, infirmities, afflictions, or troubles—many of them expecting a miracle to happen. The unbelieving and skeptical could also be seen there. Those who get in touch with Fr. Peter during his ministry for the first time react in a variety of ways. One could observe as an unbelieving, strongly built man would suddenly "collapse" under the gentle touch of Fr. Peter's hand holding a crucifix with the relics of the Servite saints (Seven Holy Founders', St. Peregrine's, St. Juliana's, and St. Philip Benizi's) only to rise up after several minutes of Resting in the Holy Spirit. One could also see as some people mustered all their strength trying to keep their stiff position so as to prove that they "would not fall down."

Miraculous healings (some of them supported by reliable medical records) did take place, indeed. Miracles are experienced by those who appreciate the miraculous nature of life, ie, as a miraculous phenomenon in itself, and who surrender to it and submit to living it out, exercising strong faith, forgiveness (for oneself and others), love (of God, the neighbor, and oneself), trust in God's Power and Grace, total devotion and embracement of God's Will, and full opening of hearts to accept whatever God will send down upon them. This allows them a "touch" of God's Love, Grace, and Mercy; as a result, they may experience an expected miracle. Fr. Peter's prayers reinforce that "touch." He himself considers offering his intercessional prayers to be his mission—especially prayers for the healing of souls and reuniting them with God by the power of Christ. According to Father, it is not the visible, physical healing that is the most important here but that which is happening invisibly and internally, and which manifests itself in the emotional, psychological, and spiritual changes—changes that turn unbelieving or cynical people into being devoted to God in full love and faith; changes that do not necessarily follow with an immediately visible mark of a miracle.

Fr. Peter himself experienced a miraculous restoration of his eyesight, which he had lost while he was a child—in a doctor's opinion—irreversibly, after sustaining an injury to his both eyes in wake of a firework explosion. He became a priest (on May 17, 1941) to fulfill a promise that he had made to God while he had been asking Him to bring back his eyesight—for, otherwise, "how could he become a priest?"

In 1948, his prayers for and blessings given to the faithful in Ireland, where he was residing, brought miraculous healings on many occasions. Despite his protests against being called "a healer," such an opinion about him was spread and his fame grew. Evidence of miraculous healings following his prayers was often documented. Upon a recommendation from his superiors wary about the increasingly growing, immense popularity of Fr. Peter, his ministry of healing the sick was ceased in 1953. Fr. Rookey received a new job. The prior of Benburb, Ireland, was made the Assistant General of the Servite Order in Rome, Italy (Harold Fickett, *The Living Christ: The Extraordinary Lives of Today's Spiritual Heroes.* New York, NY; Doubleday: 2002; p. 31). Efficacy of his prayers was considered by Fr. Peter as an unquestionable Gift of God, but—following Padre Pio's advice, with whom he met in person—Fr. Peter maintained strict obedience to his superiors. In 1986, his service was reinstated. As opposed to the name of "the healer," often coined to him by the faithful, Fr. Peter does not credit himself with any merit in this regard, because—as he constantly points out and repeats—the final healing comes always and exclusively by the Will and Power of God.

Whenever asked an often recurring question about how he feels about some people's great expectations of healing that actually go unfulfilled, Fr. Peter invariably answers: "Because the healing does not depend on myself, I cannot feel liable if it does not occur. The Divine Grace is a genuine mystery. I only pray with faith in God and love of people; the rest depends exclusively upon God. The greatest healing that a person can experience is becoming like Christ Himself, and only God knows best in what manner and when to change/heal a human soul."

At the present time of such a great demand for kindness, brave faith, service to the neighbor, love, and sainthood, it is inspiring to meet with such priests as Fr. Peter. They are one of many examples of the innumerable ways in which God reveals his caring love for us. In our times, we perceive ever and ever increasingly how far chaos, evil, and suffering can permeate all the spheres of our lives; how much at a loss we feel more and more frequently; and how much even the measuring of time becomes warped and twisted—oftentimes single days seem very, very long and exhausting, while weeks, months and, especially, years zoom by at a terrific speed.

Father Peter was born on October 12, 1916, during the First World War, and 1 year before the outbreak of the Russian Bolshevik October Revolution. So he is only . . . 88 years young. His mother was Irish, and his father had French and Irish roots. (Whenever asked about his origin, Fr. Peter often quips in a manner so representative of his individual sense of humor: "I'm both Irish and French, although I take some vitamins to 'balance' some deficiency in my being French.") His pastoral seniority spans over 64 years of priesthood, during which—and thanks to which, indeed—numerous people have drawn closer to God and have received countless Divine Graces. His service has been a nourishment for the weakened faith in many people, enlivening their faith and enriching their souls. All the gifts that God had once bestowed upon Fr. Peter have been, and still are, relentlessly shared by him with people who need them; he shares them just like Christ expected and continues to expect of His Apostles.

. . . I no longer call you slaves, because a slave does not know what his master is doing. I have called you friends, because I have told you everything I have heard from my Father (Jn 15:15). And Fr. Peter has been sharing, with all of us, what he has received from God—his faith, wisdom, truth, light, peace, gentleness, leniency, understanding, hope, compassion, kindness, and love.

It was not you who chose me, but I who chose you and appointed you to go and bear fruit that will remain, so that whatever you ask the Father in my name he may give you (Jn 15:16). And Fr. Peter has sacrificed his entire priestly life so that, through his own prayers, he could ask Our Lord to help us out in our ailments, suffering, predicaments, worries, misfortunes, or adversities. And God has made his ministry fruitful beyond all measure.

. . . No slave is greater than his master. If they persecuted me, they will also persecute you (Jn 15:20) *. . . I gave them Your word, and the world hated them, because they do not belong to the world any more than I belong to the world . . . Consecrate them in the truth. Your word is truth. As you sent me into the world, so I sent them into the world. And I consecrate myself for them, so that they also may be consecrated in truth* (Jn 17:14-19). And Fr. Peter has been delivering to us the Word of God, the Divine Truth, all with his supreme ardor and love—the highest level of love, love equal for **all** people, ie, *Agape*. He endows people with that love regardless of whether this love is reciprocal or not; whether it meets with indifference or even—sometimes—with enmity. And he gives out this love always and everywhere; in joyful situations (which he shares with everyone) as much as in those situations when his life is sometimes marked by his own version of *Via Dolorosa* (which he shares with Christ only) on his *Via Mystica*.

Always cheerful, open-hearted, with his inseparably warm look and indefatigable optimism; a storyteller, a master at wordplay and badinage, he seizes every opportunity to magnetically attract even the most unattractable. Having imposed upon himself an iron discipline, he eats one meal daily since he believes that fasting and praying heighten the effectiveness of his mediation for others. He preaches the Gospels largely by heart; he inserts facetious elements into his homilies so as to keep the congregation from "falling asleep" and make them feel about him as "one of their own." At times, there may happen to be present somebody (usually someone listening to his sermon for the first time) who gets somewhat confounded by what he has just heard and noticeably reacts by a sudden stiffening of this posture . . . and wondering if he really got into the "right" place.

The moment of the Eucharistic Consecration is the holiest communion with Christ in the form of Bread and Wine. In addition to repeatedly participating in his Holy Masses celebrated in big churches, I had the privilege of participating in a Mass celebrated by him in his tiny little chapel next to his office. I read and heard about many persons for whom it was given to see the Visage of Christ in the Host during the Eucharistic Consecration. I have never experienced that myself. On that day I stood one step away from the altar behind which Fr. Peter was celebrating a Holy Mass—the altar, at the foot of which there were laid piles of incoming letters with requests for prayers. During the Consecration, I briefly moved my eyes from the Host—which he just raised up—toward his face. All I could see then were only the eyes of Fr. Peter—as a matter of fact, what I saw were not his physical eyes; it rather was his eyes' transformation into an immeasurable suffering, an overwhelming pain that penetrated the Host and fell upon my heart as a distant—in terms of time and space—living reflection of Gethsemane . . . . I have never seen anybody's eyes changed in such an expressive exhibition of both surrendering to and suffering together with Christ . . . .

Every spare moment that he has is measured with praying on his inseparable rosary held in his hand. Every person whom he meets senses his charism right on the spot. An indefatigable pilgrim to the farthest recesses of the earth—both sacral and common—he touches the lives of many people who then long for him to return. A true Shepherd of Souls, full of reticence and humility, kissing with the same respect, not seldom with genuflection, the hand of a cardinal as much as that of a newly ordained young priest.

As a Servant of Mary, he took an oath of poverty, chastity, and obedience. His clothes do not consist of many pieces for changing and are usually "worn-out." Among the numerous presents that he receives, there is no shortage of elegant garments, but Fr. Peter can hardly ever be seen wearing them. Upon receiving a gift or a donation, which he acknowledges with words of sincere gratitude and genuine admiration for its value, he then almost immediately gives it away to someone "for whom it will be more useful" or "who is more in need." His typical personal luggage used during his trips (both domestic and overseas) is a plain plastic shopping bag with the contents not exceeding . . . 2 lb in weight plus a satchel—a worn-out leather bag filled with books, letters, articles on current religious issues, and Medjugorje messages. The satchel usually exceeds the weight of . . . 20 lb. This reverse proportion reflected in the weight of the two "parts" of his travel luggage is not a gauge of his contrariness; it is simply a reflection of his system of priorities.

To be in the presence of priests like Fr. Peter means to receive many graces. The peace, love, and light that they share with others seem to be their Natural Tabernacle, in which they live all the time on a special invitation from God as His Elect and to which they attract other faithful persons. The 2004 Polish pilgrimage to the Holy Land organized by Ewa Jurasz (of *Echo Maryi Królowej Pokoju [The Echo of Mary the Queen of Peace]*) and spiritually guided by Fr. Mirosław Wróbel, PhD, and Fr. Zdzisław Grochal—a pilgrimage in which Fr. Peter was also participating—is a good example. Since the moment of the first meeting with the group, there had been formed, and continued to be throughout the whole trip, a family atmosphere as found among the children of God who understand one another, regardless of what experiences from the past or the present they might have. Being part of a group with such priests feels like coming back home after a long absence from close family members. You "enter" such a group and become totally and immediately immersed in the proximity of feelings, matters, or problems that can be heard about or felt by the heart. Nobody had any difficulty in getting into contact with Fr. Peter, even though he was not speaking Polish, and a part of the group did not speak English. It was the same way in Poland during Fr. Peter's short post-Holy Land pilgrimage stopover there. Anywhere he was invited—be it the Piarist Fathers in Kraków (Fr. Tomasz Jedruch, the Superior, and Fr. Stanisław Kania, the publisher of a book about Fr. Peter, *Man of Miracles*) or a prayer group led by Fr. Tadeusz Kiersztyn, or private persons—he made himself at home in all those places, and everybody invariably felt as if it were a reunion and not a first meeting. He was very moved and uplifted having seen Polish churches filled with the faithful. Making an onomastic reference to the Holy Land, he now calls Poland "Holy PoLand."

Fr. Peter accepted with jubilation an invitation from the Jesuit Fathers (Fr. Mieczysław Łusiak, SJ, in Bydgoszcz) and the Piarist Fathers (Fr. Tomasz Jedruch, SP, in Kraków) to visit Poland in December 10 through 21, 2004. When earlier that year (May 2004) he was celebrating his 63rd anniversary of his priesthood in Chicago, Illinois, the event curiously coincided with the fact that many of the greetings cards that he received had as their motto the following quotation from the Holy Scriptures: *Well done, my good and faithful servant* (Mt 25:21).

Father Peter is coming to meet with his Brethren and Sisters in Poland with his open heart—to serve them well and faithfully. The true laborer of the Harvest in the Lord's Vineyard. The more we open up our hearts to the Lord, the more of His Love, Beauty, Light, Peace, and Truth will descend upon us through meetings with Fr. Peter and prayers shared.

Prepared by Barbara Wojtowicz
before Fr. Peter's visit to Poland

FR. PETER MARY ROOKEY: A SERVANT OF MARY (BASED ON MATERIALS PROVIDED BY JAMES HRECHKO, FR. ROOKEY'S ASSISTANT)

The Servite Order (the Servants of Mary) was founded in Florence, Italy, in 1233 by seven merchants, after Our Lady had appeared to them and asked for such an order to be established. The names of the founders are as follows: Alexis, Amideus, Bonajuncta, Bonfilius, Hugh, Manettus, and Sostene.

For Fr. Peter, MARY is not a dream; She is **REALITY.**

Compassion is recognized as a characteristic of the Servants *who continue to follow in their life the example of the Mother of God* (Servite Constitution article 52).

In our committment of Service, the figure of Mary at the foot of the cross shall be our model. Since the Son of Man is still being crucified in His brothers and sisters, we Servants of His Mother wish to be with Her at the foot of the countless crosses, in order to bring comfort and redemptive cooperation (Servite Constitution article 319).

Fr. Peter stands at the foot of these crosses very actively. *Christ's ambassador, a joyful Servant, a beloved priest for legions of the faithful around the world, an ideal Servant*—these are only a few of the innumerable 'names' coined to him wherever he goes.

The healing ministry is often misunderstood by many people. It is so because we do not quite understand the sense of suffering, which is one of the great mysteries in the life of Christians. We do not know why God allows suffering to be part and parcel of our lives. However, we do know that God loves us very dearly and beyond our comprehension. In the message of the Queen of Peace from Medjugorje (of September 11, 1986) we read the following:

Dear children! For these days while you are joyfully celebrating the cross, I desire that your cross also would be a joy for you. Especially, dear children, pray that you may be able to accept sickness and suffering with love the way Jesus accepted them. Only that way shall I be able with joy to give out to you the graces and healings which Jesus is permitting me.

God bestows upon some persons the gift of miraculous healing. He works through those persons to show many kinds of healing. These cures are often spiritual in nature; sometimes they are emotional and sometimes they are physical. God wants to be asked by us. It may be done by our prayers and through the prayers of other people. Our Lady makes us aware of a certain, so frequent, phenomenon:

. . . God can give you everything that you seek from Him. But you seek God only when sicknesses, problems and difficulties come to you and you think that God is far from you and is not listening and does not hear your prayers. No, dear children, that is not the truth. When you are far from God, you cannot receive graces because you do not seek them with a firm faith. Day by day, I am praying for you, and I want to draw you ever more near to God, but I cannot if you don't want it. Therefore, dear children put your life in God's hands (the message of January 25th, 1988).

And this does not sound like a recommendation; this sounds like a plea.

Why God heals some persons and does not heal some other persons is a mystery known only to Him. The fact that a person experiences some visible healing does not mean that God loves that particular person more than another who—as we would have it—does not experience the healing. The healing takes different forms, and the lack of visible physical signs does not mean a lack of God's Grace, because His Grace may appear as another, not immediately visible, gift.

An essential element of the healing to take place is the strong faith in an individual person. Also, if someone does not become healed of some disease in a visible manner, it does not mean then that the person is of weak faith or a nonbeliever. Again, this is part of the mystery of suffering and a mystery 'veiling' the gift of healing. God expects from us to have strong belief in His kindness and power. We, in turn, should allow God to act in us according to His own Will, because only He knows what is best for us. We should open up to God completely, with total surrender of our will to His Will, unreservedly relying on His Wisdom and Love. And we should do this with full faith, trust, and love, as we are constantly instructed by the Queen of Peace at Medjugorje:

Dear children! I am calling you to that love which is loyal and pleasing to God. Little children, love bears everything bitter and difficult for the sake of Jesus who is love. Therefore, dear children, pray that God come to your aid, not however according to your desire, but according to His love. Surrender yourself to God so that He may heal you, console you and forgive everything inside you which is a hindrance on the way of love. In this way God can move your life, and you will grow in love. Dear children, glorify God with a hymn of love so that God's love may be able to grow in you day by day to its fullness (the message of June 25th, 1988).

The Holy Masses for the intention of healing the sick through the ministry of Fr. Peter in the presence of people filled with faith, love, and trust are a great spiritual experience. Being together with other people (sharing the same faith and expectations) under the spiritual guidance of such priests as Fr. Peter creates an atmosphere and condition in which healing by God can take place.

Fr. Peter is a modest, kind, sincere, and deeply spiritual priest conscious of his own human nature and conscious of a great need for the Divine Grace and prayers for his intentions. After his healing ministry had been reinstated in 1986, following the 33-year hiatus (details are given in the book by H. Parsons *Man of Miracles*), he carried on his activity through the International Compassion

Ministry, operating from different monasteries of the Servants for 4 years, until he found a permanent place to set up his "office." It happened in 1990, thanks to receiving a charitable offer of renting a quiet 3-room suite for a reasonable fee in Olympia Fields in the suburbs of Chicago.

The office is run by James Hrechko ("the right hand" of Fr. Peter) and aided by secretaries Vicki Gutierrez and Sabina Reyes (with a number of volunteers—some voluntering daily, some 2 or 3 days a week, and some whenever they can free themselves). They receive numerous telephone calls to Fr. Peter and even more numerous letters with requests for intercessional prayers as well as with testimonies about the graces received thanks to Father's prayers.

Our mission—as we read in the "Mission of International Compassion Ministry"—*is evangelization and catechesis . . . Servites focus on the Passion of Jesus (the Suffering Servant) and the compassion of Mary (His Sorrowful Mother). Their 'Yes' said to God brought about His Resurrection, Her Assumption, and, for all of us, the restorative Redemption . . . The Life, the Passion, the Death, and the Resurrection are the inseparable elements of the Liturgy which makes these perpetual events present for us . . . . In our service the Holy Mass is the most essential; it is followed by the laying on of hands as recommended by Our Lord . . . We concentrate, first of all, on the internal healing.*

The charismatic Holy Masses for the intention of healing the sick usually gather many faithful. The masses are followed by the Exposition of the Most Holy Sacrament, and Fr. Peter begins laying of his hands on those who come forward to receive the blessing. They also receive the blessing with a special crucifix containing the relics of the Servite saints. Many people experience Resting in the Holy Spirit. For many of them it is the beginning of the healing process.

How many people are healed thanks to Fr. Peter's ministry? The files with incoming letters in his office in Olympia Fields burst in the seams. There have been a great variety of testimonies—from an Australian healed of bone cancer to the son of a member of the British Parliament cured of AIDS. Many testimonies refer to the cases of healing painful experiences from the past or recovering from the spiritual imbalance after many years of torment.

Most of the people coming to the Holy Masses for the intention of healing the sick expect a miracle to happen. However, Fr. Peter emphasizes that "in this (earthly) life, we will never be completely healthy." He also adds that "the suffering and the healing are going together in pair. If we proclaim the words that exclude the spiritual value of the suffering, then Christ does not speak through us. If we proclaim the words that exclude the healing by God, then this is not the Gospel of Christ."

Elaborated by Barbara Wojtowicz
before Fr. Peter's visit to Poland

II

POLAND, DECEMBER 10-21, 2004:
THE ITINERARY OF THE
VISIT AND ILLUSTRATIONS

. . . Jesus warned them sternly, 'See that no one knows about this.'
But they went out and spread word of him through all that land.
(Mt 9:30-31)

BYDGOSZCZ

December 10
* Arrival at the Fellowship of the Jesuit Fathers at the St. Andrew Bobola Parish

* Visit to the Oncological Hospital

* Visit to the Order of the Discalced Carmelite Sisters, Tryszczyn

December 11
* Visit to the Rehabilitation Ward of Dr Jurasz' Clinical Hospital

* A Prayer Meeting with the Padre Pio Prayer Group
  (led by the Fathers of the Capuchin Friars Minor)

* Chaplet of the Divine Mercy and the The Holy Mass evening at the Jesuit Fathers Church

December 12
* Celebration of a Holy Mass in the Church of the Capuchin Friars Minor and a visit to the Cloister of the Order of Capuchin Friars Minor

* Holy Masses celebrated at the Jesuit Fathers Church

December 13
* Visit to the penitentiary

WARSZAWA

December 13
* A Rosary Prayer and a Holy Mass concelebrated at the Sanctuary of Our Lady the Educatrix of the Youth in custody of the Piarist Fathers

December 14
* A visit to the Pulmonary Disease Ward, Warszawa Municipal Hospital

ŁOWICZ

December 14
* A Rosary Prayer and a Holy Mass concelebrated at the local Church of the Piarist Fathers

RZESZÓW

December 15
* A Rosary Prayer and a Holy Mass concelebrated at the local Church of the Piarist Fathers

KRAKÓW

December 16
* A Rosary Prayer and a Holy Mass concelebrated at the local Church of the Piarist Fathers

December 17
* A meeting with the Easter 2004 Group of Polish Pilgrims of "The Queen of Peace" to the Holy Land

JASŁO

December 17
* A Rosary Prayer and a Holy Mass concelebrated at the local Church of the Piarist Fathers

KRAKÓW

December 19
* Sunday Masses concelebrated at the local Church of the Piarist Fathers

December 20
* A Holy Mass concelebrated at the Sisters of the Divine Mercy Chapel in Łagiewniki and a meeting with the Sisters and guests

December 21
* A Holy Mass in the Piarist Fathers' Chapel before the departure to Chicago

Deeply moved, Fr. Peter Mary is greeted by Fr. Dabrowski, a chaplain, and a group of young people singing *We welcome you, Alleluja!* at the entrance to the Oncological Hospital in Bydgoszcz, Poland.

A Holy Mass is offered in the Oncological Hospital chapel in the presence of patients and their family members.

Visit to the Order of the Discalced Carmelite Sisters in Tryszczyn (District of Bydgoszcz); Fr. Peter Mary autographs the Sisters' cards.

Blessings are given to the Carmelite Sisters by Fr. Peter Mary.

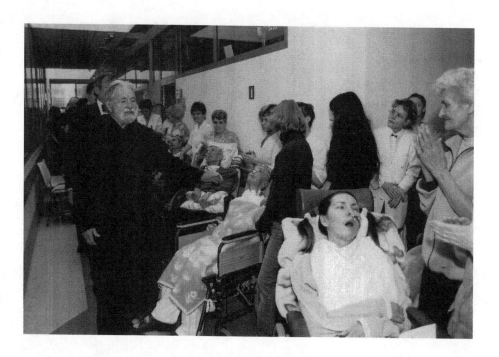

Visit to the Rehabilitation Ward of Dr. Jurasz' Clinic in Bydgoszcz.

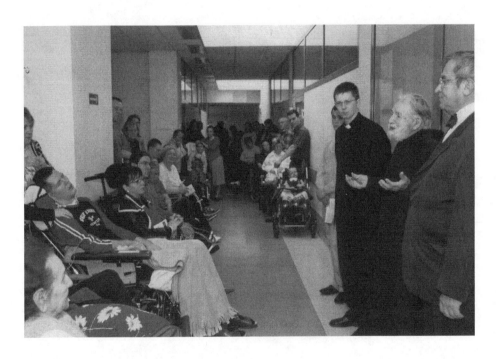

Fr. Peter Mary blesses the patients accompanied by their family members.

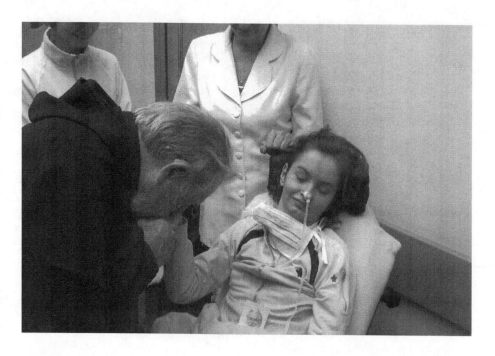

Fr. Peter Mary kisses a comatose patient's hand, expressing his deep compassion.

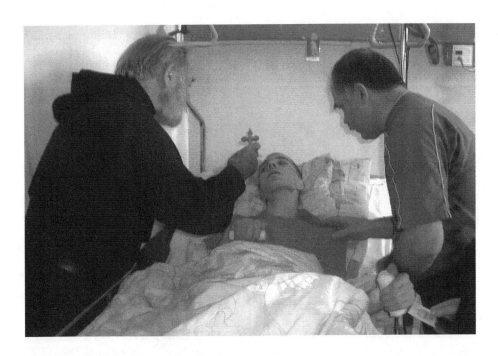

Fr. Peter Mary prays over a comatose patient, Radek Dzierzbicki, who sustained severe injuries in a car accident, including trauma to his brainstem and a pierced lung. Radek began to wake up from his coma shortly after Father's visit and was released home.

A meeting with the Padre Pio Prayer Group in the little Sanctuary of the Virgin Mary at Oplawiec (District of Bydgoszcz). Father, assisted by a local interpreter Piotr Bocian, talks to the gathered faithful.

Fr. Peter Mary prays over one of the participants of the meeting.

Jesuits' Church at the St. Andrew Bobola Parish (Bydgoszcz) filled with the faithful awaiting Father's arrival.

A group of Mass-concelebrating priests, with Fr. Peter Mary in the middle, ready to enter the church from the Sacristy.

A spontaneous answer to Fr. Peter Mary's welcoming *Alleluja!*

The moment before the Consecration during the Holy Mass.

Fr. Peter Mary Rookey praying prostrate before the start of the healing service following the Holy Mass.

Father's assistant, Brother Jim Hrechko, SOSM, familiarizing the faithful with Father's healing ministry, sacramentalia, and the Resting in the Holy Spirit.

Crowds of the faithful wait for Fr. Peter Mary's blessings.

Fr. Peter Mary, accompanied by a local Jesuit Father holding a Monstrance with the Eucharist, gives individual blessings to the faithful.

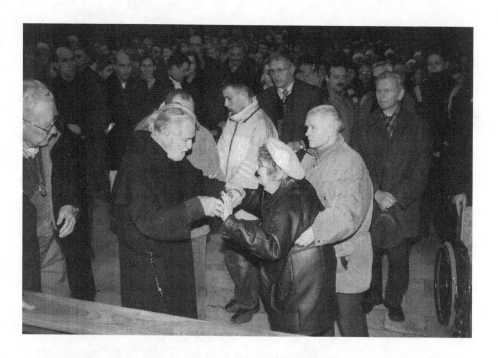

After Fr. Peter Mary's encouragement, a wheelchair-bound woman leaves her wheelchair and, supported by Father, starts to walk.

Joyful Fr. Peter Mary, assisted by Danuta Felix (local facilitator) and Fr. Rafal Kwiatkowski (Father's local interpreter) arrives at the Jesuits' Church.

While Fr. Peter Mary tirelessly gives his blessings, one (Danuta Michalowska) of the many order-keepers directs people to the line filled with those awaiting their turn.

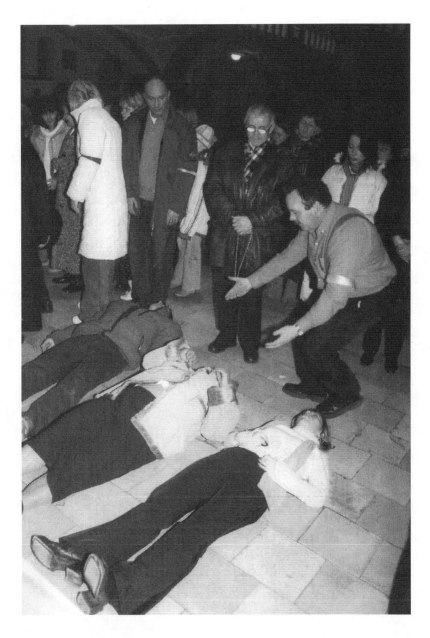

One of the "catchers" is very busy, but is even more and truly amazed with the numerous people experiencing the Resting in the Holy Spirit after a single round of blessings.

A Holy Mass is concelebrated by some local Franciscans in their Church of the Capuchin Friars Minor (Bydgoszcz).

An after-Mass gathering at the Cloister of the Order of Capuchin Friars Minor.

The interior of the Church of the Sanctuary of Our Lady the Educatrix of the Youth at Siekierki (District of Warszawa) in custody of the Piarist Fathers.

A beautiful marble statue of Our Lady behind the altar at the Sanctuary of
Our Lady the Educatrix of the Youth.

Standing closest to Our Lady's statue, Fr. Peter Mary searches for a copy of the Missalette.

Fr. Peter Mary looks for the English version in a multilingual Missalette.

Fr. Peter Mary and his local interpreter, Fr. Artur Demkowicz who translates Father's homily from English to Polish.

Fr. Peter Mary and Fr. Antoni Szlachta, whom Father had first met in the Holy Land in April 2004, surrounded by Piotr Zygier; Helena Sosnowska, who also first met Fr. Peter in the Holy Land in April 2004; and Jadwiga. All were very happy to have an opportunity to have their picture taken with Fr. Peter, just before Father left the Piarist Fathers' place for the Municipal Hospital in Warszawa.

A brief preparation, in the presence of a chaplain (Fr. Maciej), for Fr. Peter Mary's meeting with patients of the Pulmonary Disease Ward of the Municipal Hospital in Warszawa.

Top from left: Agnieszka Kaczmarczyk, Fr. Peter Mary, and Kasia Zygier; center: Danuta Lis (local coordinator of Father's meeting with patients in the Municipal Hospital), Fr. Stanislaw Kania; and four nurses (one standing and three seated) of the Pulmonary Ward personnel, just before Father left the Municipal Hospital in Warszawa for the next destination, the Piarist Fathers Church in Lowicz.

A group of priests concelebrate the Holy Mass at the
Piarist Fathers Church in Lowicz.

Fr. Peter Mary says his homily during the Holy Mass
at the Piarist Fathers Church in Lowicz.

A group of priests concelebrate the Holy Mass
at the Piarist Fathers Church in Jaslo.

A wheelchair-bound man, encouraged by Fr. Peter Mary, starts to walk, supported by Father and Urszula Uljasz (Father's local tour assistant), witnessed by Bro. Jim Hrechko, SOSM (on the left), during the healing service at the Piarist Fathers Church in Jaslo.

A group of priests concelebrate the Holy Mass at the Piarist Fathers Church in Rzeszow: The Eucharistic Celebration.

The Eucharistic Celebration: Consecration of the Wine.

Sign of Peace.

III

FATHER PETER MARY ROOKEY, OSM, WITH THE JESUIT FATHERS IN BYDGOSZCZ

The Strengthening and Revival of Faith: Fr. Peter Mary Rookey Visiting the Jesuit Fathers in Bydgoszcz

Fr. Peter Rookey's visit to our Parish was undoubtedly the most exceptional event that took place during the 4 years of my service as pastor of Saint Andrew Bobola Parish in Bydgoszcz. Exceptional was not only the fact that, until then, I had never seen in our church so many people gathered (surely in the number of more than 6000). Above all, exceptional were those peoples' spiritual experiences. Fr Peter's statements—simple and straight but uttered with a great power, followed by his so devotedly fulfilled ministry of the healing prayer over the sick—left an indelible trace in the form of strengthening and revival of faith in all the participants of the Liturgy. Until today—and I write these words 3 months after Fr. Peter's visit—many people reminisce about those events. Most (perhaps even all) of them—young and old, simple and sophisticated—were left strengthened in spirit. Even children! Personally, I cannot right now give any specific witness regarding a possible miraculous physical healing that followed Fr. Peter's intercessional prayers, but I can testify to many spiritual fruits! I am enormously grateful to the superiors of Fr. Peter for having permitted his arrival to us and, above all, I am grateful to him for having preached the Good News to us and prayed over us with such enthusiasm despite his age and, therefore, limited physical strength.

Father Peter, I am impressed by your bearing, Evangelization fervor, and faith in Christ! I would be very happy if you visited us again. After Fr. Peter's visit, we received a great number of telephone calls with the question of when he would come to us again. We pray so that this unusual event might happen in our church again.

In my own name and on behalf of the entire Community of the Jesuits in Bydgoszcz,

Fr. Mieczysław Łusiak, SJ

A Profound Testimony to the Life in God: Fr. Peter Mary Rookey in the Cloister of the Discalced Carmelite Sisters at Tryszczyn

Thanks to the intermediary Danuta Felix [a local facilitator of Fr. Peter's visit to Bydgoszcz], we were honored to entertain Fr. Peter Mary Rookey in our cloister on the day of December 10, 2004.

After his arrival in Poland, Fr. Peter Mary concelebrated the first Holy Mass in Bydgoszcz in our Chapel and, afterward, gave his blessing to the Sisters as well as the faithful gathered in the Chapel. From many persons' accounts, we know that Fr. Peter's visit left in them deep spiritual experience and good that cannot be adequately expressed with words.

Father met with us in the locutory, and we were greatly impressed by that longer, direct contact with him. For a long time will we remember Father himself, his deep spirituality, and simple lifestyle. Father eagerly answered questions asked of him by the Sisters and brought in an atmosphere of joy and open-heartedness.

We are very grateful to the organizers for this stay of Fr. Peter in our cloister. He left in us an example of his profoundly devoted life in God.

Sr. Joanna M. of St. Theresa (of Avila)
Carmel at Tryszczyn

HAVING SO LITTLE, HE HAS IT ALL: I SET ALL MY HOPE ON HIS BLESSING

By the time it reached me in a very unusual manner (through the Bernardine Sisters in Kraków on June 29, 2004), *The Miracle Prayer* had already been working miracles in my heart for several months. Every word in it was familiar to me, as it resounded within me like an echo reverberating my previously uttered prayers. Through them I, too, implored God for the miracle. I implored Him on my knees, under the Cross, kissing the feet of Jesus, flushing them with my tears. And God did hear my cry. From my humanly contaminated and continually empty hands, He accepted my most pure sacrifice and intention offered to Him in the greatest humility and love, stripped of all that was mine. The intention was very personal and resembled a voluminous novel, albeit contained in but one little word. And God, Himself being Love and Kindness, took care of everything as Good Father by sending upon me His Holy Spirit, the Comforter and a Guide. It came to me in a form of a "sign"—a picture of the Infant Jesus (also received from the Bernardine Sisters). And it was to strengthen me and lead me in a way that would enable me to see further "signs" preceding every step of mine and to avoid mistakes. And, day by day, everything changed. The flower for which I was asking changed into gardens; and a drop of water, into oceans of graces. Surely, as a human being, I will never comprehend all this. It was just like a beautiful "spiritual story" about a tiny little and quite ordinary grain of sand that was my intention very close to my heart. The intention that God turned into a beautiful, enormous and precious pearl using His Power.

Since the very start of my desire and the first prayer with the request that Fr. Peter would come to us and bless us by the Power and Will of Christ until the moment when I rested in the Holy Spirit after receiving Fr. Peter's blessing, there had been nothing that would originate within myself. I kept asking God unceasingly to take me away from myself. And the Infant Jesus—my Guide, was continually being born in my inspirations, thoughts, and acts every day again and again. The Holy Spirit's presence in all that was sensed as never before, and I was only His tool that He used, so that some be healed in their bodies, others in their souls, and yet others have theirs hearts of stone changed to hearts of flesh—all by God's Mercy and Graces.

I asked God to send us Father Rookey, because I set all my hope on His blessing. I felt deeply that Jesus and Mary would transfer that cry of mine and that desire from my heart directly to the heart of Fr. Peter who would recognize it in compliance with God's Will and would receive the Light as to how very much he was needed here. St. Padre Pio, whom Fr. Peter met personally—and who is my spiritual Father—was present in that invitation right from its inception. I felt as if Fr. Peter's visit to Poland were under Padre Pio's patronage. The invitation was sent for Fr. Peter by the Jesuit Provincial on September 23, 2004 (Padre Pio Feast Day), and then almost every place visited by Fr. Peter (Padre Pio prayer groups, the hospital wards, in which there were pictures, statues, and relics of Padre Pio) was marked by Padre Pio's constant "presence" during Fr. Peter's visit. Fr. Peter also stood at the Altar in the Little Church of the Capuchin Friars Minor and visited them at their cloister nontypically located in an apartment building.

The purity of the intention and the need for blessings from Fr. Rookey uncovered huge layers of good in people attending those meetings, and devotion and unity during the preparation for the visit, despite the occasionally rising and piling up of hindrances. And those hindrances were just mere signs telling us that we chose the right way, right because—as we know—there usually appear to be obstacles in doing good.

Many were witnesses to miracles taking place—those spectacular manifestations, necessary for people like Doubting Thomas, as well as those for whom I had asked in the solitude of my heart at everyday meetings with Lord Jesus in the Eucharist. And they occurred because God wanted it so and He loved us so much. One of the first such miracles was the waiting time for an answer to our invitation—from September 23 (the day of the dispatch; the Feast of Padre Pio) till October 7 (the day the "YES" answer was received by the Jesuit Provincial; the Feast Day of Our Lady of the Rosary), so much besought and expected through our prayers! I will never forget the atmosphere of those wonderful days, meetings, prayers full of peace, joy, and love, which accompanied Fr. Peter, and the crowds that surrounded Him everywhere. Unforgettable will also be and always alive the blessing that Fr. Peter gave me, touching my head with the Crucifix. On that Crucifix (I learned about it later from Father) Jesus' right arm is missing—but the power of that arm of Our Savior is there when Fr. Peter blesses people.

Until then, I had never met a man of so noble posture and being so available to others (except for the Holy Father John Paul II)—and available continually, despite his age. That saintly and humble Servant of Mary is a channel through which Our Lord bestows His Graces on us, listening to his intercessional prayers. Father Rookey is a reflection of freedom of a man entrenched in God and totally in love of Mary. At the start of his path to holiness, he pledged to live in poverty, so everything that he possesses, moreover, what he has on, he keeps in one small bag. And, while he has so little, he has ALL, because every heart that he touched, every name that he uttered, and every look that he bestowed became his blessing for us and for his true wealth. By giving his love—all of himself and to everyone—he receives it back evermore; so, yes, he is rich! Every heart, asking for a miracle by whispering his *Miracle Prayer* directly to the Hearts of Jesus and Mary, became changed, but changed in a way different from that in our own plans, desires, or imagining. Different because it was getting filled with some kind of God's Mystery whose Truth and Dimension will only be recognized once we move to eternity.

Father Peter will stay in my heart in a very special and loving way. I received my gift of the intercessional prayer and the prayer of the heart when asking for a miracle at the School of the Cross, at the Feet of Jesus in the Grave and on the stony paths of Mary at Medjugorje. That prayer changed my heart, whereas God's Grace given to me through the hands of Fr. Peter is a joyful solitude of the heart filled up with the Love of God. It is a state difficult to describe, but I know that God wants through this state to prepare me for something. I do not know for what exactly, and I do not know how, but the special blessing that Fr. Peter gave me rested upon me as a sign of the great Mercy of God toward me and the great confidence that God put in me by revealing to me so many areas, in which my prayers and sacrifices were in need. I feel the responsibility for the mission of apostleship, to which I was called by name by Jesus. I am now different than I was before; everything seems different to me. And, even though I still do not comprehend it, I trust that God will take care of everything. And when He Himself takes care, I need not to worry. He wants to free me and needs my "Yes." The humanly inconceivable Divine Wisdom sometimes chooses tools so fragile and cracked.

Fr. Peter has been to Medjugorje many times. He said that he felt the need to return there, as he continually wants to be Mary's student and Her servant, because Mary teaches us love, mercy, reconciliation, forgiveness, humility, standing at the foot of the Cross, and, eventually, carrying the cross. And, no matter what cross it is, we carry it always together with Our Lady of Sorrows. Jesus on the Cross opened for us His own School of Love in His Pierced Heart, from which His Blood and Water gushed out, and it is there where He commanded us to settle—at the very source of Mercy and Graces. Fr. Peter has been accompanied by both Jesus on the Cross—in the name of Whom he blesses us, and Our Lady of Sorrows—Whom he serves. He also came to visit those people whose life was marked by the cross. He came to them during the novena to Saint John of the Cross (a Carmelite monk), and it was just from the Carmelite Sisters that he began his ministry in Bydgoszcz, and he left Bydgoszcz on the Eve of the Feast Day of Saint John of Cross.

The school of humility and obedience, of listening intently to God's inspirations and not neglecting them, is often taken by some as "violence" against humanity—so difficult it is deemed to be. Since God called me by my name and showed me the way that is steadily narrowing and becoming more and more of a steep path—but the only one that leads me to Him . . . then I am taking this way. And Fr. Peter blessed me on this further way, so that love, peace, goodness, and reconciliation may always dwell in my heart, allowing me to fulfill the Holy Will of God, although—at times—I will not understand it.

In conclusion, let me quote an excerpt from "The Message of Pope John Paul II to the Young People prepared for 'World Days of the Youth' in Cologne 2005."

Mary, "Woman of the Eucharist'" and the Mother of Wisdom, support our steps, light up our choices, and teach us to love what is true, good, and beautiful. Conduct all to your Son Who, as the only One, can satisfy the innermost desires of the human heart and mind. Mary, the Seat of Wisdom, pray for us!

Father Peter Mary, nearly 10 000 hearts in Bydgoszcz only pray for you, asking God that you—if such will be His Will—may come again to us to continue to bless us, speak to us, confer peace upon us, love and teach us humility, since you yourself are Humility.

May God allow you to continue making use of the gifts that He has granted you and to carry Divine Miracles from the Hands of Jesus and Mary to people for many, many years to come. People need those miracles enormously.

Grateful to you for everything, with incessant prayer,

"Donna d"

I Seek God Everywhere and in Everything

And behold, I am with you always, until the end of the age
(Mt 28:20)

I got a copy of *The Miracle Prayer* on June 29, 2004. In my heart, I felt it as an extraordinary prayer putting us before God in the glory of the love of the Cross. It is the Cross that offers hope for us that we are not left alone in our everyday concerns, that the Lord is near and our "Yes" will suffice, and then the Merciful Love will overwhelm our lives and peace will reign in our hearts.

The joy of the soul accompanied us unceasingly ever since *The Miracle Prayer* and sharing it with others during preparation and the arrangements for the arrival of Fr. Peter. Despite various adversities that were growing out like weeds to ravage the growing flowers, the Lord surrounded us with His care and confirmed that we were on the right way. He was putting in our way some good people who provided us with their assistance and supported us with their prayers, kind words, and encouragement.

Our joy became complete when Fr. Peter arrived in our city of Bydgoszcz, and we had the opportunity to accompany him at close range. I was very moved by that, my heart felt like a garden full of flowers. Those were, indeed, some remarkable days, like being in another world, another life. The Lord is Great!!!

Fr. Peter carried his ministry to many different places: hospitals, prayer groups, and the Discalced Carmelite Sisters at Tryszczyn. All those meetings were filled with an atmosphere of jubilation and peace. The faces of the people revealed great emotions, with tears flowing down, of which nobody was ashamed. Extraordinary and full of spiritual experiences was our participation in the Holy Masses. Despite the great crowds, the Divine Order was omnipresent. There reigned the atmosphere of fervent prayer, silence, and peace; many persons were weeping tears of joy and purification.

I was one of many persons who helped keep order. While Fr. Peter was tirelessly giving his blessing with the crucifix containing the Holy Relics, I felt very tired for a moment and terrified by the upcoming crowds of people patiently waiting for their own turn. I remember that I looked up then at

Father who was moving with unusual lightness, as if levitating, and His face was youthful and radiant with joy. It gave me so much strength and verve that the sense of fatigue vanished completely, and the crowd terrified me no more. It was an unusual ministry, all the more that, for the first time in my life, my family, including my husband and some relatives, participated in such a great event. We were all very happy and will surely keep returning to those beautiful and pleasant memories.

Rejoice in the Lord always. I shall say it again: rejoice! (Phil 4:4). The meeting with Fr. Peter was, from the outset to the end, a jubilation, a Joy in the Lord!

Awake, oh north wind,
and come, oh south wind!
Blow upon my garden
Because I languish for your love.

It was exactly how I felt during the visit of Fr. Peter; my heart was overfilled with love and peace.

So very, very much do I wish to give Glory to the Lord for His unceasing going out to meet us halfway and not leaving us all alone; He gives us on this way His holy priests who lead us, light up the way for us, and speak about the immense Love of God for everyone. One of them is Fr. Peter Mary Rookey—a humble and loving Servant of God's Mother. Father Peter became a light on my way. He is quiet, humble, full of love for the Crucified Jesus and for compassionate Mary, and of brotherly love for every person he comes in contact with. Thanks to that nobody could feel 'worse' or less important. His engaging sense of humor; his good eyes in which the beauty of the deep side of his soul was visible—all that touched me very deeply. I can only deplore my meager vocabulary and that I cannot fully express what I really experienced in the sanctuary of my soul . . .

All I know is one thing, I became different. The Lord changed me. I seek God everywhere and in everything. Where I do not find Him, my heart is seized with great sadness. This transformation is so great that I myself cannot comprehend it.

The Lord says: *all that you ask for in prayer, believe that you will receive it and it shall be yours* (Mk 11:24). My everyday meetings with the Lord and the Mother of God in the Eucharist and at prayer became a source of life, strength, light, and desire for the union with the Most Holy Trinity, and to search for God's Will and its fulfillment. My heart wishes one thing—the Glory of God in all!

Dear Father Peter, I will not come up with anything unique in my words of thanks for your great service to God and I will join up with many thousands of people who, exactly like I do, love you very much in Jesus Christ for what you do.

May the following words, which I had once heard, be an expression of the change I have experienced and a reflection of what I feel in the depth of my soul.

> *I decided to follow Jesus*
> *I decided to follow Jesus*
> *I will not go back anymore*
> *I will not go back anymore*
> *Though in solitude*
> *I will continue to go on further*
> *I will not go back anymore*
> *The Cross is ahead of me,*
> *The world is left behind me*
> *I will not go back anymore.*

"Donna m"

OVERJOYED WITH *THE MIRACLE PRAYER*

In my priestly work, I give myself up to people. Conversations and meetings take a lot of my time. Because of that I neglected reading or learning by heart, which, anyway, had not come to me easily lately. Before the arrival of Fr. Peter Mary Rookey, I left to lead an Ignatian retreat. During its course, something occurred at night that caused me to feel some neural pain in an area of the hip joint in the morning. I tried doing some exercises, but the pain, instead of passing, became stronger. I had to leave the retreat attendants and return to Bydgoszcz to seek medical help. In the evening, I could move no longer. The medicines that I was taking did not work; the night was terribly difficult to bear.

On the second day I decided to read a book about Fr. Peter translated into Polish. Earlier on, I had also heard a negative opinion of a certain person who had called me and asked whether the Jesuits realized whom they had invited and that he [Fr. Peter] "was practicing magic, healing over the telephone, etc."

The Miracle Prayer hit me straight off. I sensed that it was a prayer of my heart. I decided to learn it by heart. As I mentioned above, my memory was not in its best service to me at that time. And here I am lying on my side, feeling the pain, yet repeating the words persistently. I was surprised that, practically within one moment, I had succeeded to master the text of that prayer. Since then, I have been saying *The Miracle Prayer* day in and day out; often more frequently than once a day. Limited by the disease, I celebrated Holy Masses in the household chapel with students who came in to help me with the preparation for the Eucharist. We said this prayer every time—either at the beginning or in the latter part of the Mass—offering it for the intention of Fr. Peter's arrival and those who would be coming for healing.

All suspicions and anxieties sown by persons opposed to Fr. Peter's arrival receded, and I decided to join the ARKA Ministry Group in their preparation for the meeting. There were many telephone calls and a great deal of confusion. Primarily, the meeting was designed to be for spiritual renewal groups in Bydgoszcz. It turned out, however, that the community organized buses from other cities. We began to worry whether there would be enough room for all of them in the church. We, first of all, invited them to come to the last Holy Mass on Sunday. Next, worries came up on Sunday when the pause between the first and the second Eucharist was too short for Fr. Peter to give blessings to all who gathered. We were stunned to find out that every Holy Mass, despite the crowds of attending faithful, ended 15 minutes before the beginning of the next one. There was no rough and tumble or any need for medical intervention. Everything passed on in harmony and peace. The workings of the Holy Spirit were perceptible; He managed it all. I am deeply convinced that *The Miracle Prayer* prepared us for submission to the Holy Spirit.

Dear Father Peter—a beloved disciple of Christ! I thank you in my name and on behalf of my students for the words of your *Miracle Prayer*. It helps us stand up before God, which is so very important, and to which St. Ignatius encourages us so strongly to do through his own spirituality. He tells us to realize our standing in the presence of God before starting every meditation. Thank you, God, for the grace of the meeting with you, Father, for the strengthening of our faith, and for the joy that you left among the weary people. You were teaching us to confide in God. We were uplifted by your humility, poverty, and zeal in serving other people. I hope that this was not our last meeting with you, Father. I commend myself to your prayers, Father. May you continue to be such an obedient tool in the Hand of Our Lord.

Fr. Piotr Idziak, SJ

My Service to the Servant of Mary

It all began one evening, when, on returning home after work, I dropped in for a moment to see my parents and check out things. My mother informed me then about an upcoming visit of a certain priest from Chicago who was healing people. In the first moment, after hearing that, I thought that the priest would be a quack. In the next statement, my mother came up with a question, "Would you agree to interpret for that priest?" My general lack of time and daily bustle pressured me to say "No," but the faith and hope for some possible improvement of my condition, which I read from her eyes, made me say "Yes" in response.

Afterward, the preparations for Father's visit ensued, including settlements with the tour planner. I insisted every time that, should there be a greater number of volunteer interpreters, I would prefer to be treated as the last one on the list—not that I wanted to avoid performing as an interpreter, to which I had given my prior consent, but because I was in doubt as to whether my scanty knowledge of the prayers and biblical texts in their English-language version would permit me to provide a good service for the pilgrim priest. Despite my excuses, I felt—guessing the Lord's ways—that this role would fall on me anyway. And so it did.

I began to prepare for the meeting with Fr. Peter by reading a book about him, concerning his ministry. I devoted much of my time studying that book to get a deeper familiarity with its hero whom I was about to serve. Page after page, Fr. Peter Mary Rookey, the priest from Chicago who was unknown to me earlier, grew in my eyes. When I halfway read the book, I felt very honored, chosen, by the fact that my modest knowledge and skills would be able to serve him. Fr. Peter's view of the world appealed to me and, most important, enriched— indeed, educated—my point of view. Every opportunity to make us wiser is extremely precious, since wisdom makes people just. The true revelation I found in the book was the written argumentation on the subject of the admittance of the spiritual, physical, and emotional healing of a person who neither wants it nor believes in it. Fr. Peter points to the superior authority, the omnipotence of the Lord God who chooses and decides all by Himself about the fate of man. One of the quoted examples referred to St. Paul. A point of view similar to Fr.

Peter's allows us to see hope for those people who have lost their faith, who no longer have the desire to live, and who act as if they have burned their bridges after them. Fortunately, this does not mean they have separated themselves from God to the point that He cannot reach them. It also allows us to remain humble and, consequently, prevent one from feeling better than those who do not obey the God-given Ten Commandments; for really, one does not know when and who will be touched by the Divine Grace.

Interesting, Fr. Peter had not arrived yet and, still being faraway, he was already complementing my views with his attitude and deeds described in that book.

The day of Fr. Peter's arrival came double quick. My everyday duties and work—often involving me in excess—were the reason why the time had passed so fast despite a 2-month anticipation of his coming. So, finally, there came the date of December 11, 2004—the day of my first meeting with Fr. Peter. I went to the Dr Jurasz Hospital in Bydgoszcz, where Fr. Peter had a meeting with the sick. Already being in the hospital, I was heading down the hallway on the way to the ward in which Father had a meeting. When I took the last turn, I saw a throng of diseased people in their wheelchairs, on their beds, standing, sitting, and Fr. Peter among them. From the distance, I looked on the faces of all those people and what they were expressing could be described as joy, hope, and peace. No doubt it was just the presence of Fr. Peter that had evoked such feelings in those persons. At seeing God's actions delivered upon other people through this humble priest from Chicago, I felt my jitter intensify, realizing that I would have to serve a true Servant of God and Mary.

After the meeting, I was introduced to Father and exchanged some words with him. At close range, I was able to confirm how very nice, full of joy, warmth, and peace that priest was. The next event of his 4-day tense visit was a meeting with the faithful in the little Sanctuary of the Virgin Mary at Opławiec (district of Bydgoszcz), during which I was supposed to interpret. And, again, I saw a great hope and joy in the people waiting there—so immense that one could almost be made speechless under the impression. That [speechlessness] happened to me once or twice while translating. It made Fr. Peter give me a light poke straight off, just to bring me back to my senses. It really must have looked funny—somewhat like a grandfather who wants his diffident grandson to do his best. Of course, he did not fail to express a couple of nice words about me during his speech. At the end, Fr. Peter gave his blessings to all the gathered people. Many of them rested in the Holy Spirit. The atmosphere of the whole meeting was very uplifting and festive; it is difficult to describe this hope, trust, and full devotion of the sick in particular. I experienced them as an example and an instruction for us; there were persons with ill bodies but with firm value systems; they were not inclined to the pursuit of a career, knowledge, money, or performance rating—certainly because they put God in the first place. Subsequently, every moment that I spent with Father bore a fruit of deep reflection.

The next meeting with Fr. Peter was on the same day during the Holy Mass celebrated at the church of the Jesuit Fathers. I came to that Mass together with my dear wife. The church was filled up with a crowd of faithful pilgrims from all over the country who came to the Mass. Somebody else interpreted for Father then, so I had a time for quiet prayer and meditation. During the Holy Mass, just like during the preceding meetings, the overwhelming feeling of joy, hope, and peace was dominant. Father Peter in a split second won the hearts of the participants with his sermons, which were occasionally 'peppered' with subtle humor. During the blessing, again many people rested in the Holy Spirit. It was amazing to be able to observe a Servant of Mary as an intermediary between the faithful and God. The man going between us and God—a real Servant of Mary. Many believers called Fr. Peter directly a saint, to which he answered, "Oh! I know myself and I know that . . . it is not so."

Deeply touching was also Fr. Peter's ministry in a prison, where he prayed with the inmates and gave them his blessings. By his attitude, Fr. Peter showed how we ought to treat another person, regardless of his/her actual circumstances. Father Peter aroused and strengthened within the prisoners a true desire to work on themselves. When the prisoners were expressing their gratitude to Father for his visiting them, he answered them beautifully that it were they who were his benefactors, because—by inviting him—they made it possible for him to visit God Himself who dwells in them. He was really happy to be able to serve the needy by the pursuance of the Bible, *I was in prison and you visited me*. Father Peter may be compared to a well from which we can drink water on and on. I am glad that God favors His own servants so very much; it is then easier for us to go to Him through such servants.

Father's stay in Poland was a splendid and unique retreat that bore fruitful crops. One of them was my liberation from the rush of the commonplaceness.

Until Father's arrival, my busy regimen was wearing me out both physically and mentally. It was but a continuous pursuit of something that is generally thought of as "good." My professional and scientific work, my engineering projects—such an amount of work to do everywhere that, even working with no or limited sleep, one probably would not be able to cope with it in a timely manner. Suddenly, I realized that overworking myself was putting a heavy strain on me. I go by the rule that the time for prayer should be lengthened in parallel to the growing number of activities and, especially, in proportion to increasing success of any kind. Steadily drifting away from implementing that rule, I realized that it was a sign for me that accumulated activities were drawing me away from God, and that was a great danger. "And when we will be in our sleep, may even our sleep praise You"—my sleep had not been giving praise to God. I was falling down as if thunderstruck from exhaustion, waking up in the morning, and so on and on like that. Being overworked also diminishes the ability of concentration during prayer, this way making it empty. I was getting an impression of being confined inside some shell or enclosure. I compared myself to a massive train running over the tracks in the wrong direction and nothing, and nobody was in a position to turn over the switch and change its wrong course. The invisible pressure of the satanic rush of the day-to-day commonplaceness, only to be deprived of the time for God, due to whatever—fatigue, success, defeat, desire of knowledge, money or the lack of it. God broke this shell, using Fr. Peter, and turned the switch over on my tracks, and set me free from that continuous rush. And for that I am especially grateful. Once more God showed me His own omnipotence. To tell the truth, I have not quit being involved in my activities, but I have extended the time of performing them and changed my attitude toward them.

Those three days of Fr. Peter's presence revealed an image of higher values—calmness, contemplation, and fasting; an image that left unforgettable spiritual experiences inside me. Most of all, I am happy that I could serve the Servant of God and Mary, listen intently to his words, observe his ways, and learn from him how to pray. I wish to work over my own faith and perfect it, following the example of humility embodied in Fr. Peter, the priest from Chicago.

Piotr B.

A Highly Emotional Welcome

Our prayers were heard. On December 10, just after his arrival in Bydgoszcz, Fr. Peter Mary Rookey came to us by a small van. As soon as he appeared in front of the hospital building, we gave him a hearty welcome. A small group of young people, accompanied by guitar, sang a greeting song and, afterward, followed our guest all the way to the chapel already filled to the brim with sick people. Profound emotions were visible on all faces. Our guest also melted into tears at such an affectionate welcome.

In his speech, Fr. Peter reminded us of the words of Good News from the Letter of St. Paul concerning healing. He implied to us that Jesus was near the ill and unwell. We also received the grace of being anointed with blessed oil by Fr. Peter. All along, we were coming up for the blessing in a file, all focused and singing songs. Fr. Peter's words gave us so much hope! All of us received a small picture from Fr. Peter with the text of his *Miracle Prayer* and a rosary, as well as encouragement to say this prayer with faith every day—because it is just the strong faith that is the most necessary for a healing to take place.

Thanks be to God the Highest who granted us such a gift that Fr. Peter could come to the oncological hospital. We thank Fr. Arkadiusz who finally gave his permission for Father's visit. This visit will stay in our hearts for a long time.

Monika

WHERE PAIN AND SUFFERING WERE DOMINANT, AN ADMIRABLE JOY AND HOPE TOOK OVER

Friday, December 10, 2004, was a special day in the Oncological Center in Bydgoszcz—marked not only in the history of the hospital but also in the history of our city.

I am a frequent guest at the hospital due to my service of singing and playing music during the Eucharist. In the afternoon hours of the preceding day, I found out that—along with several persons from a Spiritual Renewal community named "Carrying the Spirit," affiliated with the Saint Matthew Parish—I would have an opportunity to participate in this unusual service to be officiated by the 88-year-old Rev. Peter Mary Rookey from the USA, who has a special gift of healing prayer for curing people of cancer and other diseases.

We were waiting for the meeting in great jubilation. The Chaplain, Fr. Arkadiusz Dąbrowski, a man deeply concerned about the well-being of the patients and the entire hospital, took care of the necessary preparations and the setting of this beautiful event. Not being able to come at 3:00 PM, several persons from the community came much earlier at noontime to adore Lord Jesus in the hospital chapel with communal prayer and singing. It was a very joyful and Holy Spirit-inspired time preceding the arrival of the Guest. A couple minutes before 3:00 PM, we went down to the entrance of the hospital to greet him with singing. When he appeared, Monika, a sister from the community, a joyful mother expecting her first child, intoned to the accompaniment of a guitar a song *We Welcome You, Alleluia!* Then we sang another song, *Welcome Our Guest*, and, singing out, we led Father, along with the newly arrived accompaniers, onto the upper storey of the hospital to the conference room for a small treat and a short conversation. Next, we went to the hospital chapel, where he was awaited by many patients, a group of several doctors, and other persons committed by Fr. Arkadiusz to the service of his beloved sick.

At the beginning, Fr. Peter greeted everyone very warmly and began his prayer of worship of God and *The Miracle Prayer*, which he encouraged everyone to say every day, irrespective of the current state of one's health.

After reading out a fragment of St. Mark's Gospel (Mk 16:15-18), he began to anoint with the Blessed Oil every participant of the service. During anointing, the whole chapel and the Pilgrim's Nave resounded with glory to God by singing: *Sing Alleluia to the Lord, Let There Be Glory and Honor and Worship,* and *Let's Praise the Lord for He Is Good.* It was amazing that, in the place where usually pain, fear, and great suffering reigned entirely, an admirable all-embracing joy and hope took over.

Father said that many among the ill would see soon that they became healed in some way and that something would change in their lives. If the healing process would not have been visibly complete on the outside, then it would certainly come inside. The unusual simplicity, joy, and modesty in Fr. Peter make people desire to be near him. That was particularly discernible in the warm and cordial reception Father was given by Fr. Arkadiusz, who embraced him several times.

After the conclusion of the service and giving thanks, we sang together the songs: *Black Madonna,* and *Since Very Long Thou Have Been the Queen of Poland.* Father Peter, however, asked for a yet another song, which turned out to be the worldwide popular *Gospa*—a song from Medjugorje. So, we bid a singing farewell to Father and his entourage.

When most of the persons taking part in the prayer meeting had left the chapel, the group of the Spiritual Renewal, along with the young people invited by Fr. Arkadiusz to help the sick, continued to sing in joyful exultation a song to the Glory of Christ who, like 2000 years ago, had shown us all His immense Mercy in this special place by bending over one man who had been ill for thirty-eight years who had no one to put him into the pool when the water was stirred up (Jn 5:1-8).

Wioletta B.

Praying With Fr. Peter Mary Rookey
at the Oncological Hospital Chapel

Invited by the Jesuits, Fr. Peter Mary Rookey, "man of miracles" from the USA, stayed in Bydgoszcz on December 10 through 12, 2004. Immediately after his arrival in Poland, he came to the Oncology Center Hospital. He received there a hearty welcome by the Chaplain, Fr. Arkadiusz Dąbrowski, members of the Spiritual Renewal community, and evangelization youths from the basilica. Led by those persons greeting him with singing, he entered the hospital building. After taking a short rest, he got to the Chapel of the Divine Mercy. Here, he fell on his knees before the Holy Sacrament in great humility. His presence and prayer evoked in me, a participant of that meeting, deep reflections that I would like to share herein.

First, the sprinkling with holy water reminded me of the Grace of Baptism and that this gift was for my protection, to ward off evil spirits.

Second, *The Miracle Prayer* made me aware that I had:

* to stand in humility before God and be conscious of my own littleness and powerlessness,
* to apologize to the Lord for my sins and ask for His forgiveness,
* to pardon all those who have wronged me,
* to set myself free from the power of the evil,
* to totally surrender myself to God and invite Him into my own life,
* to implore God The Father through the most precious Blood of Jesus for the healing of my soul, senses and body,
* to utter within my heart that I love the Lord Jesus, thank Him for everything, and desire to follow Him, and,
* to turn to the Mother of God, my Patron Saints, and the Angels.

Third, the words of Lord Jesus directed to His disciples gathered on the Mount of Olives before His Ascension (Mk 16: 13-18), quoted by Fr Peter, reminded me that

* priests go to all the corners of the world preaching the Gospel and baptizing—if I am baptized and accept with faith the Christ in the preached word, then the way to salvation opens up for me,
* those who have faith will be accompanied by various signs like, among other things, "hands will be laid on the sick, and they will be healed"—I asked myself if I believed that the Lord enables priests for ministry and makes them His own tools—as Fr. Peter himself had emphasized that he was merely **a tool** in the hand of the Lord.

Fourth, a fragment from the Letter of Saint James the Apostle (said by Father)—*Is anyone among you sick? He should summon the presbyters of the church, and they should pray over him and anoint (him) with oil in the name of the Lord, and the prayer of faith will save the sick person, and the Lord will raise him up. If he has committed any sins, he will be forgiven* (James 5:14-15)—inspired me:

* to trust God completely,
* to "put my stakes" with Jesus and to confide in Him completely, and,
* to look for strengthening in prayer in times of sickness and suffering, because only Jesus is the healer of the body and soul.

Fifth, the prayer by Fr. Peter, his anointing with the Blessed Oil, and the blessing received from him drove my thoughts to the Word of God.

Fr. Peter's advanced age, his humility, calmness, gentleness, love, and the expression of his eyes made me see in him an image of Christ and himself being His tool.

Adam Barej

A Faint Glimmer in the Tunnel

For sick persons, a diagnosis "it's a cancer" is often equal to a death sentence. As an effect, most people who have cancer lose their sense of life and any hope for a better tomorrow. And, after all, to overcome any kind of disease, we need to have faith and think positively.

On December 10, 2004, many patients at the Oncology Center in Bydgoszcz saw a faint glimmer light up in the tunnel. On that day, Fr. Peter Mary Rookey held a prayer service dedicated to the cure of the sick on the request of Fr. Arkadiusz. It was an unspeakable experience for everyone gathered. I felt favored very much, when I had a badge put on me with an inscription "assistant" on it and was allowed to greet the guest from America with joyful singing. Fr. Peter was deeply moved by the young peoples' singing, the sound of guitars, and the sick people smiling. However, most important to him were the sick who gathered in crowds in the chapel. The communal saying *The Miracle Prayer*, the anointment and the blessings given by Fr. Peter let them persevere until the end of the service despite their pain and suffering that they were bearing.

I do not believe that any of us will forget that afternoon. I hope that many from among those sick will be healed of cancer. And I am convinced that every soul was healed and re-filled with faith, hope, and love.

Joanna Jasinska

THE DAY I SAW FR. PETER MARY I WILL REMEMBER FOR THE REST OF MY LIFE

First of all, I would like to voice my concern about whether my story should rather stay within my heart and mind only. Would this not be haughtiness and a lack of due humility before God and the Blessed Mother on my part? Because I thought to myself, 'Why could I experience such a Grace? Aren't there many people loving God above all, ready to succumb to His Will beyond limits and fear? And I?' I am a believer, but surely not to such a degree as even my dear wife, for example. The fact is, and I am fully aware of it, that many people prayed very hard for my recovery, ie, my family members, friends, priests, and many other persons. But it comes as a rule that we turn to God in times of hardship and fear.

The days of December 7 through 22, 2004, were spent by me at the Oncology Center in Bydgoszcz. I needed an immediate treatment of some neoplastic changes on my skin. My condition was very grave, as the doctors—at least some of them—rather had not promised anything good, based on their prognosis due to the state of my illness at the time of my previous hospitalization. As they were used to putting it bluntly, they "saw it all in dark colors," referring to my medical condition on the day of my admission to the first hospital as well as on the day of my discharge from that hospital. I guess one can only imagine what my state of mind could have been after hearing such statements, after having seen all the changes on my skin, and having had frequent hemorrhages through cracked arterioles.

I must also admit that, back at home, I completely entrusted myself to the Blessed Mother and kept asking Her all along for help and the intercession to Her Son Jesus Christ. I even painted a copy of Our Lady of the Scapular—an image at our church at Brusy. I wanted to have the same image as the one at the church with me every day. I believed that it would be the Mother of God only who would bring back my ability to enjoy life and allow me to have my part in raising my 4-year-old son.

When I was admitted to the Oncology Center in Bydgoszcz, my first step in getting familiar with that place was to find the chapel. As early as on the first day, I participated in a Holy Mass. I was fascinated by the atmosphere of the place—unusually friendly toward everyone present—and by the priest celebrating the Holy Mass, Fr. Arkadiusz. He exuded some uncanny warmth and love for every person—be it a believer or somebody lost. In the chapel, I felt the love of God given to all patients through the person of the priest who was present there.

When I found out from Fr. Arkadiusz, after just 4 days of my stay in the Center, that we would be visited by Fr. Peter Mary Rookey, I accepted that in a rather normal way. I did not even think that that monk would be able to help me one way or another. I came to the chapel—as I was accustomed to everyday—for the Holy Mass, with a rosary in my hand, to pray and ask the Most Glorious Virgin to take care of me and other sick people, and for her to intercede to Her Son Jesus Christ. My faith that I would obtain the help and the intercession of the Mother of God was growing stronger and stronger in me; my pleading with Our Lady was becoming more and more fervent and zealous. Throughout my prayer, right in front of my eyes just over my head, I saw a picture of Our Lady adorned in a gray and blue robe, with her hands extending in my direction. Lightness in the form of dispersing rays was coming out from her whole figure. I think that it was my own artistic vision (since I am a painter), considering my predisposition for the arts and my acquired creative imagination. Nevertheless, it allowed me to pray more fully and, in a way, to have a conversation with the Blessed Mother.

I prayed by saying "Hail Mary" decades of the rosary practically everywhere: during irradiations, while waiting for lamp therapy sessions or doctors' visits, in leisure time, in the hospital chapel—everywhere.

The day I saw Fr. Peter Mary I will remember for the rest of my life. And so, just like all others who, on that day, came to the chapel, I was waiting for Fr. Peter's arrival. When he arrived, Fr. Arkadiusz introduced him briefly and the service started. Throughout the service, I listened attentively to the translations of Fr. Peter's prayers. At the high point, if one may call it so—at the moment when Fr. Peter was blessing everyone with the Cross with relics held in his hand, I suddenly felt some very strong burning in the area of my body affected by cancer. I had a sensation as if somebody had suddenly touched the stricken area with a scalding hot iron. I instantly felt very weak and realized that I was close to fainting. So, I sat down on the bench at the corner of the chapel and was kind of turned off from reality for a moment. Some other patients from my ward who were in the chapel had had to have noticed it, because they immediately started to ask me questions as if something had happened to me and whether I was fainting. After a while, the feeling of weakness passed and the burning sensation in the cancer-affected area disappeared as well.

I must sincerely confess here that what had happened to me was—by no means—thought by me as something exceptional at that particular moment. I was thinking that it was the result of a myocardial infarction, which I had had back in June 2004. Only what followed the next days allowed me to believe that it had been Our Lady's intervention. Oh, yes! I believe in that, and it will stay so until the end of my days. I felt something dying in my belly, something that had made me unable to live a normal life before. Apparently, my breathing improved, I could eat normally, sit up, and walk. The nurses who were changing the dressings on the affected parts of my skin everyday also said that the wound was cleansing itself, the healing process had started, and became clearly noticeable to them, too.

As soon as I left the Center, I started to analyze everything in details; and all the facts, one by one, began to arrange themselves in a logical sequence, undoubtedly willed and directed by "Somebody." Namely:

1. If I had not been in the hospital for the heart failure that I had in June one year earlier, I surely would not have undergone the cancer treatment in the Bydgoszcz hospital then and, even if I had, it would certainly have been too late.
2. My treatment was postponed by the clinic in Gdań sk (to this day, they have not called me for the lamp therapy).
3. My later admission to the Oncology Center in Bydgoszcz, where Doctor Ziolkowska made the only right decision (a brave one, I will add) with a bit of disbelief in its success.
4. In the "Case Summary" section of the hospital discharge chart, the doctors stated the following:
    . . . Despite an extensive and advanced stage of local ulcerations and leaking fetid pus and bloody content out of the lesional skin of the lower aspect of the abdomen, an attempt to treat it with irradiation was made . . .—It indicates that the doctors themselves did not quite believe in the success of the treatment modality they used "**despite** . . . ." This, too, in my opinion of course, is indicative of the Divine intervention.
5. A follow-up visit at RCO (Regional Center of Oncology) in Doctor Ziólkowska's office 3 weeks later showed that the cancerous lesion, which had the size of 23 cm x 20 cm on the day of my discharge from the hospital, was healing, leaving a small crusty wound of the size of 6 cm x 4 cm.
6. Today, February 9, 2005, only a very little part of the once huge wound remains in the previously cancer-affected area. There is no pain, inflammation in the wound, or other discomfort.

All that I have listed herein is what I remember as having had gone through. There is not even a bit of untruth or my own invention, or fancy in this written account. The interpretation of this testimony and the granting or not granting of credibility to my words are up to Father Peter's and competent persons' judgment.

Praise be to Jesus Christ and Mary, the Eternal Virgin!

Marek Blech

I Heard the Voice in My Heart . . .

My meeting with Father Peter Mary Rookey was a source of an uncommon experience. When I came to a 12:30 PM Sunday Mass for healing the sick, concelebrated by Fr. Peter, I was directed to the balcony. I was glad, because I could see everything better from an elevated level. I saw Fr. Peter only at the end of the Holy Mass. I had a slip with prayer intentions from persons who, not being able to come themselves, asked me to pray for their healing. I also added a request for blessings and graces for all the priests of our parish church, enclosing the names of some of them.

Yet on my way to the church, I had asked Our Lady to accept all those intentions and present them to the Lord Jesus, because I would not have the time to say them or would forget some of them. I listened to the Holy Mass intently, and a thought that I would surely experience Resting in the Holy Spirit kept returning to my mind. I received Holy Communion and knelt down to adore Jesus. I spoke to Him, "Lord Jesus, there is nobody stronger than You; You are the greatest Power; Lord, You are the Almighty One!" But it lasted only briefly. I got up to sing. Then something strange happened. I felt some internal urge to kneel down again, which I did and worshipped Jesus in my heart, with all my soul, extremely fervently.

All that passed. Then I saw Fr. Peter by the altar. The priest presiding over the meeting announced that, apart from Fr. Peter's blessing, there would also be given a blessing with the Eucharistic Body of the Lord Jesus in the Monstrance. I said to Lord Jesus again, while walking up for the blessing: "Lord Jesus, You are the only and the greatest Healer, the Almighty One." I received the blessing of the hands of Fr. Peter and the one with the Eucharistic Body of Christ. I did not rest in the Holy Spirit.

When I was returning home, I heard a voice in my heart: *You see, I used the priestly hands to deliver My Graces, not only the hands of Father Peter; the Monstrance was also held by the priest. I always bless you through the hands of priests, either in the Holy Sacraments given by them or in other ways. The priests are My tools.*

Through the hands of the priests, Lord Jesus sends us the greatest outpourings of His Graces of Mercy and Love in the Sacrament of Reconciliation. All I have to do is bend my head humbly and ask for those graces and thank Him for them with my heart.

Today I say Fr. Peter Mary Rookey's *Miracle Prayer* for the intercession of Our Lady, the Lord's Saints, and the Guardian Angel. My life is changing slowly. My faith is becoming deeper. I believe that Jesus is in my heart and that the priests are His chosen souls.

Thanks! The Worship and the Glory for everything to the Lord! Thank You Lord Jesus for Father Peter and all the priests of our Church. I am sorry, my Lord, for every wavering in my faith.

Wanda

My Heart Would Like to Beat Within the Heart of God Himself

*Saint Anthony, teach me humility and patience, fortitude and courage
so that I may persevere and never fall away from the Crucified Jesus.*

In hindsight, across the several weeks that have passed since the visit of Fr. Peter Rookey in Bydgoszcz, I can say today without hesitation that it was a great honor for me to meet him, get to know him, and accompany him on his way and throughout his ministry in Bydgoszcz. Above all, however, it was a time of great grace for me and for the thousands of other people like me. Father Peter arrived in Bydgoszcz, the city not known to too many people abroad, with its name so hard to pronounce by any non-Polish-speaking person that barely a few may find it easy to pronounce it properly.

I had not known Fr. Rookey nor had I heard about him until December 2004. Today, however, I know that the graces that the Good God sheds on people through his hands had touched me much earlier on. God adopts the way of patience and humility. He likes to take us by surprise. So I was taken by another surprise just a couple days ago when I received a letter from a person who had been supporting me with a quiet and persistent prayer, a prayer full of faith and, so full of power on my way to the priesthood and at my first parish in distant Canada. In her letter, she wrote me that she had rested in the Holy Spirit after receiving a blessing from Fr. Rookey on a pilgrimage to Medjugorje in 1995!

However, when Fr. Rookey visited our city, I had not the slightest idea what possibly to expect. I can now confirm that he came here to make present—among us, pilgrims on this earth—the great works and miracles of Jesus Christ Himself! Many of them have not been recognized by us yet, and we can know nothing about them for a long time, until the right moment comes. He came to us with his ministry. He came humble and full of trust, based strongly on Mary, to cause God's Power and Life to become part of the life of the people who need Him so very much. And, then, He, our Lord and Savior, would grant them "the Water of Life" that is purity, a light attracting man, and being life itself. And it happened so, and I witnessed it all, and I have experienced it till today.

I am a diocesan priest and—thanks to God's ruling and thanks to the people whom He has put on my way of life in the most unforeseeable ways possible—I have had the tremendous privilege of participating in most of the services and prayers for the healing of the sick. It was not the first time, then, that I was taking part in this kind of prayer meeting. But what I saw with my very eyes, what I experienced in the inmost depth of my heart, and what I have been going through until now, surpassed my most daring imagination and expectations. Words fail me as I try to adequately express and describe all the existing reality of God's presence. Those several days of communal prayers with Fr. Rookey were a time of a great feast of faith, of people raptured by God and desiring to surrender themselves to the burning fire of His Love. For many people, it was a moment of awakening in their faith thanks to the prayer and presence of Our Lord Jesus Christ. I saw that miracle happen! For others, it was an experience of the strengthening of their faith. For us all, those were the moments, in which we tangibly experienced the living presence of Jesus in the faith of the Church community. I saw the miracles and great things happening before my eyes, and all that thanks to the charisms that the Lord has deigned to lavishly bestow on Fr. Rookey.

Until this moment, many people from among my parishioners who took part in the Holy Masses and prayers for healing the sick come to me to share with me how much they experienced the recuperative and life-changing presence of Jesus and the supernatural peace that can only come from the Holy Spirit. They say that their lives are no longer as they had been until then and that they have changed.

Personally, I can also testify that my life has become different, anew. I am not anymore the way I had been until December 10, 2004. I experienced a spiritual healing that manifested itself on several levels. I was relieved from irritations and temptations, which were like a festering wound that dwelt within me for many years and remained eradicable. I experienced in fullness what it means to know Truth being Jesus liberating us from the dark power of evil and sin so that we may be the Children of Light. All that by the matter of an extraordinary blessing that Jesus gave me through the hands of this giant of faith and prayer—Fr. Rookey. Ever since the time of those splendid days, prayer has become the only thirst of my soul, and my heart would like to beat within the heart of God Himself. I am too poor in words to express how much the intensity and depth of my meeting with Jesus in the Eucharist has increased—with Him Who is the beginning and the end of the entire created world, and Who has turned my heart—meager and stony—into a heart of flesh. In my soul, in all my life, the spring has arrived. I long to feel its first blossoming flowers. I have a deep foreboding that there is some important purpose behind this, about which I can know nothing as of today. But I believe that, soon, I will recognize the meaning of all those twisting and turning paths leading me from the little parish of St. Joseph at Kentville, Canada, through the Church of St. Jarvis in Paris, France, until this evening at the Church of Saint Andrew Bobola in Bydgoszcz, Poland, and the meetings of the men burnt out crazy for God.

With his blessing, Fr. Rookey brought upon me, and us all, the works of God's Mercy. He did it as a quiet and lowly son of Mary. His face emanates kindness and peace, care for the salvation of man, and the Love of the Crucified Jesus. Father Rookey is a person who is replete with divine subtlety and human fragility woven with the elements of sainthood that make him a priest who follows the way of Christ to show this way for us all in bright light. How vast is within him the resemblance to Mother Theresa. Just like she, he is an extension of the Merciful Hand of God who embraces us with kindness, forgiveness, love, and peace—how different from all that is offered by the world.

Dear Father Rookey, I thank you for your presence among us, for having come to give us your witness about Christ and pull us onto His way—the way of trusting and fulfillment of God's Will with all my life, the way very difficult but how joyful. Thanks to you—Dear Father Rookey—now, I am not afraid to pray with these words:

> *Father, I abandon myself into your hands;*
> *Do with me what You will.*
> *Whatever You may do, I thank You.*
> *I am ready for all, I accept all.*
> *Let only your Will be done in me*
> *and in all creatures.*
> *I wish no more than this, O Lord.*
> [Charles de Foucauld's prayer]

Written on the remembrance day of St. Anthony, the Abbott, January 17, AD 2005

Fr. R.K.

THE CHURCH WALLS WERE NOT 100-YEAR-OLD BUILDING MURALS BUT THE PEOPLE UNITED IN PRAYER

Some time has passed already since the memorable and impressively fruitful visit of Fr. Peter Mary Rookey in Bydgoszcz. Make no bones about it, I did not expect that it would arouse in me such a great excitement and sense of God's closeness, as well as the power of the Holy Spirit.

I consider myself a normal and ordinary Catholic, who lives in compliance with the Christian traditions derived from my parents and through religious catecheses at church. I try to live my life in agreement with the rules of my religion and my own conscience. It appears to me that Jesus rewards me for this by giving me an opportunity to have a quiet and worthy life. I have a splendid family, three children, a job, good health, and financial stability, so I am inclined to maintain that I am favored by God's Grace. One could say that I need nothing more, that I have all for which many people pray fervently.

However, like all people, I am being put to a variety of tests in my life. In his/her life, everyone is challenged by difficulties and problems both personal and familial. Thanks to prayer and faith in Divine Mercy, I succeed in overcoming predicaments. Perhaps I am the kind of man who does not put up the challenge level for himself too high and is happy with everything that he is given in his life and takes it as it is willed by God and—on the other hand—treats life's difficult or tragic situations as a test of his faith. It seems to me that looking at life in such a way gives me the peace of mind, and my faith in the good gives me a sense of security.

However, I have never felt so filled with joy and love as on those memorable days when I was taking part in the Holy Masses and prayers with Father Peter in Bydgoszcz. I felt honored to have an opportunity to help keep order and serve as a "catcher" during Father Peter's ministry. It is hard to understand how what I saw and how I felt then at the church really happened.

Before Father Peter's arrival, everybody was encouraging me to read the book by Heather Parsons titled *Man of Miracles* that would prepare me and answer many questions related to the power of Jesus and the Holy Spirit, as well as the role of Father Peter in acts of reconciliation. I read the book shortly before Father's arrival in our city, and I was under a strong impression of what it described. The events about which I learned seemed to me unlikely. The cases of healing and the so-called Resting in the Holy Spirit seemed possible, but not to such an extent as I then would personally observe them during the communal prayer at a number of the Holy Masses celebrated in Bydgoszcz.

The atmosphere at the church was extraordinary. For the first time in my life, I participated in the prayers and the Holy Masses for hours and I did not feel the passing of time and had no sense of fatigue or tiredness ever setting in. The congregated people came for the most part to get help with their problems and to become healed. Probably not all of them were then aware of what was about to happen in that church. Being very close to the altar, I could observe the behavior of many people who, all surprised, were approaching Fr. Peter to receive his blessing. I could notice the expression on their faces on seeing—probably for the first time ever—the persons who stood very close to them falling and Resting in the Holy Spirit. Not expecting such things to happen, those people themselves did not suppose that they, too, could receive this Grace. Seeing and putting down on the church floor many persons experiencing the Resting in the Holy Spirit during the blessing, I could not believe that its occurrence could be taking place on such a mass scale.

This Grace was experienced by people young and old, short and tall, the haves and have-nots (judging by their appearance), the priests, and altar boys. That was amazing! I felt the lightness of those people who were falling down automatically onto the floor as well as the power of the Holy Spirit passing through them toward me, giving tingles to my body at the moment when I was arranging the people on the floor. The expression of their faces testified that they were happy at that moment, and so they surely were. In some persons standing close by, I saw a kind of envy toward those who had received that grace personally. But I also met with some cases of people who had received the Grace only after having several meetings with Fr. Peter, after showing persistence in participating in the services and prayers for a miracle. I also saw the joy and crying of an elderly woman who got up from a wheelchair after receiving a blessing and passed a several-yard distance by the altar.

But there was also a situation where a small girl resisted her mother's strong efforts and desire and screamed not wanting to approach Fr. Peter to get a blessing, as if the power of his kindness were . . . unnaturally feared by her.

The atmosphere of that living church was unique. Having been right at the center of those astounding events, I felt that, at that time, the real walls of the church were not the church building's 100-year-old murals, but all those people united in prayer. One can rarely feel something of that kind, but it was so then.

I also personally experienced the Grace of Resting in the Holy Spirit after the blessing ending the last Holy Mass on that day. I really felt then the sensation of being in a state of semiconsciousness, in which the world outside ceases to matter, and the mind becomes quiet as if it were running into a state of calmness and wished to stay in this state as long as possible. Such moments can really change you. Through those several days, during which I took part in the prayers and in the Holy Masses, my faith underwent a considerable transformation. I am ashamed to admit that, but until then I had been unable to see the power of the Lord Jesus and the Holy Spirit in a dimension about which I had not known. I am happy that my eyes opened up to what was so close, but which I had not seen until then.

The Grace of Resting in the Holy Spirit that I experienced is a sign that Lord Jesus is all along close by me, is watching over me, and helps me in straightening the ways of my earthly life so that I may be able to reach eternal life.

Father Rookey is a wonderful link in my reaching Jesus. He shares out the power given to him by God with great love and a sense of fulfillment of the splendid duty. The mission that he fulfills gives people hope and makes them return to strong faith, which nowadays is very hard to find.

I hope that God will still continue to grant Father Peter good health so that he be able to carry on enlarging the family of God, which has often gone astray.

Wojtek W.

THE LORD IS WAITING FOR ME UNCEASINGLY

To describe what I experienced from the Lord through the hands of Fr. Peter, I must first say something about myself.

I am a believer; however, I live in a nonsacramental relationship and, unfortunately, nothing can change this now. I am married to my present husband by registry only, because I am not allowed to have a church wedding, having once been in a sacramental marriage with another man. My husband is a very good man. He is a good husband and a good father. We have lived together for 12 years, and we have four children. We raise them in the Catholic faith. They attend a Catholic school and belong to the Eucharistic Movement of the Young. They are very much into the life of the Church. We are proud that we bring them up this way. I mention this to sketch the situation of our family.

However, what I miss at every Holy Mass is the possibility to receive the Lord in the Holy Communion. I incessantly find myself guilty of my husband not being allowed to receive the Lord into his heart. I plead with God in all my prayers to let me and my husband confess our sins before we die and receive Him into our hearts. Yes, I do receive Jesus at every Holy Mass spiritually. But only He knows how much I envy those who can go up and take Him "physically" into their hearts.

Being so overwhelmed with the sense of guilt, I wondered if God really loves me, if I deserve His love, if He sees my struggling, if He hears me out. Living in such uncertainty, I found out about Fr. Peter's arrival in Bydgoszcz. I heard that he would be concelebrating Holy Masses for the intention of healing the sick, that he would be blessing everybody after every Holy Mass. I thought to myself that I was not sick and I would not go to those Masses. Besides, my husband was not at home and my going to a 3.5-hour Holy Mass with my 3-year-old twins would be almost 'suicidal.' However, the Divine Providence watches over my family. If the Lord decides on something, we only have to agree. Jesus did decide that I had to be there at the healing Mass with my children.

On Sunday, the first thing in the morning, my mother came to me and said that she had attended a Holy Mass with Fr. Peter on the preceding day and that

I had to go there, too. Her key argument was the fact that the twins had been coughing badly for 3 months, probably from allergy, and 8-year-old Irmina was sick all the time and she had already been hospitalized twice that year. I decided to go. But how would my preschool kids hold out for 3.5 hours at the church when, on a 40-minute Sunday Mass they blow up the church to pieces?

First, what surprised me, was the fact that the twins were sitting spellbound, looking intently into the altar, with their little hands folded up. Although we had come 10 minutes before the beginning of the Holy Mass, we were lucky to be given very convenient seats on the balcony of the already overcrowded church. Impossible, is it not?—As if reserved just specially for my children and me, with an unobscured view of the altar. My preschool children could see everything perfectly well. Father Peter did not concelebrate that Holy Mass; he only had the sermon; his just being there was sufficient. His presence was sensed, and the calmness that emanated from him enthralled everyone. It could be felt how much his heart was overfilled with love for Jesus and Mary and for every person.

The time spent at the church passed so quickly! In fact, all too quickly! Nobody felt bored; no one could by any means become detached from experiencing the Holy Mass. Praying was bringing thoughts about God only. And everybody was highly focused and engrossed in prayer.

Right from the start of Fr. Peter's service, my mother took the twins and, together with some other children, approached Fr. Peter to receive his blessing. Father Peter folded his hands, swayed his head, smiled, and blessed them. I saw it all perfectly well from the balcony; it crossed my mind that he knew what kind of urchins they were.

I was standing in a line together with my older children waiting patiently for our turn. After a long wait, a gentleman from the order maintenance service finally approached us but there was enough space for my children only. I continued to wait more patiently, because the Lord wanted me to do so. First, my children; then I. After receiving the blessing, the people were leaving the church through the side door, unless they received the Grace of Resting in the Holy Spirit, in which case they were calmly lying on the church floor until they "awakened." When my children went out, it was my turn. Standing in line and waiting for the blessing, we prayed and sang songs all along. And here I am, standing up in front of Fr. Peter. I feel that he is a man of God, chosen by God. The only thought I have is that I want to see him at close range and look into his eyes. Suddenly, I see the other priest holding the Monstrance with the Lord Jesus and blessing me. I bow my head before the Lord instinctively and no longer see anything. I feel overcome by great joy; I feel as good as never before; I feel great calm. I want this moment to last eternally.

The Lord gave me the Grace of Resting in the Holy Spirit. I did not see Fr. Peter's face, his eyes; I did not see him at all. But, after all, that was not the most important. He is only a messenger; the Lord acts through his hands. When I woke up, the feeling of joy and peace stayed on. I wanted to pray; I wanted to do it very much; I had so much strength within me and, at the same time, I was full of the peace of Christ. I knew it—that was the answer to my doubts. The Lord is with me, the Lord loves me, and the Lord is unceasingly waiting for me. From now on everything depends on me. I can go together with Him through all my life. He gave me a foretaste of what awaits me in eternity. I have a choice and free will.

When my husband called me up in the evening and I told him about everything, he said: "You will see that the twins will stop coughing." They did, and allergy tests showed that they were not allergic to anything. Since that time, Irmina has never fallen ill and she even goes to the swimming pool. I regained my peace of mind, and I know that Jesus is always with me. He cares for all my family. He listens to everybody, only we do not know how to talk to Him. He answers to everyone, only we do not know how to listen to Him.

Thank you, Lord, for Fr. Peter. I understood so much. You strengthened my faith so much.

Justyna

THE "GANGSTER" FROM CHICAGO VISITING THE PRISONERS IN BYDGOSZCZ

In the Fall 2004, information began to spread by mouth that, upon an invitation from the Jesuit Fathers, an extraordinary "healer" priest was coming to Bydgoszcz, one who prayed a lot and ate only once a day. That did not make any particular impression on me; after all, I receive the Body of Jesus Christ Himself at every Holy Mass. Only reading a book titled *Man of Miracles* opened my heart to Fr. Peter's charism. I started to read that book and—after a dozen or so pages—I just was reading how Father prayed for gangsters at a cemetery in Chicago, and all along I was peeking at my watch because I was to go, together with the ARKA Fellowship, to a weekly evangelization meeting at a prison in Bydgoszcz. At each meeting there we say the Chaplet to the Divine Mercy, the Rosary, we read the Bible; there is a catechesis and, of course, communal singing to the tune of a guitar. I took the book about Father Peter and photocopies of *The Miracle Prayer* with a photo of Father for every participant of the meeting.

The prayer meeting was very fruitful. Every detail of the life of Father was absorbed by the inmates—about those eyes of his severely damaged, which were healed by Jesus in reply to the faith of Fr. Peter's mother, her storming of Heaven using the most beautiful prayer—the Rosary; about his absolute obedience to the Church (on the advice of Padre Pio), also at times when his healing ministry was stopped; and about his memory in prayer of those who ruled the city slightly differently—the way of . . . Al Capone . . .

We all said *The Miracle Prayer* entrusting to God and the Immaculate Virgin our own injuries, and each of us especially commended "that single problem of his or her," which was in his or her heart.

Our brethren desired to participate in a Holy Mass at the Jesuits' church to receive Fr. Peter's blessing. In answer, we could only say this: "Pray, because the Lord can do everything."

Two weeks later, Fr. Peter Rookey and accompaniers came to the prison for a meeting with the convicted. The apprehension was huge, because copies of the book about Father had been circulating among the prisoners and it was known that Father's blessing is often accompanied by Resting in the Holy Spirit. The prisoners were waiting for it subconsciously and I analyzed, with some anxiety, a variety of possible scenarios of events, for example, involving the prison guards, the convicted, the invited guests, or the helpers experiencing "the Resting." Allowedly, this is a place with stepped up discipline and, besides, the prisoners who belong to the prison elite will not even touch the mugs of their fellow inmates, to say nothing of a situation in which one would have to provide any kind of support for another.

The Lord had a different plan. Resting in the Holy Spirit during the blessing was received by some of the "outside" people accompanying Fr. Peter, while the remaining people, inmates included, continued saying the Rosary.

Father Peter excelled everyone with his greeting: "Praise be to Jesus Christ! I am a gangster from Chicago; I left my own Colt in the States." Some delicate smiles appeared on the faces; the ice was broken. Later on, he told the prisoners, in a very interesting manner, about the triple denial of Peter the Apostle, whose name he himself was bearing, about various prisons, and, above all, about St. Paul imprisoned in Rome, and about St. Maximilian in the Nazi Death Camp at Auschwitz.

At the next meetings, we remembered the words of Fr. Peter about the last moments of St. Maximilian's life, when he gave his rosary made of bread to the person sent down to make a lethal injection on him, and to whom he said: "Take it, it'll lead you to Heaven." That person underwent a deep conversion and was present at Saint Peter's Square in Rome during the celebration of St. Maximilian's canonization. The prisoners were sharing their own personal experiences. There were some among them who received tangible graces.

Father did not have enough time to visit other prisons, in which we—as a foundation of the Institute of St. Brother Albert—hold cyclical evangelization meetings among male and female inmates in Koronowo, Inowrocław, Grudziądz. Instead, in all these prisons, we distributed *The Miracle Prayer* among the inmates being under our "charge," encouraging them to say it every day. Whole meetings were dedicated to Fr. Peter's ministry. In Grudziądz, the prayer was preceded by a testimony of a mother who forgave her son's murderers.

It is harder to reach those who resent God. At Koronowo, we have an inmate named Paweł—he does not seek any guilt within himself but maintains that it is the Lord always "taking on him." At the meetings, he often behaves as a "devil's advocate." Lately, when he was leaving after one of the meetings with ARKA, I asked him casually if he perhaps would like to read the book titled *Man of Miracles,* adding: "an interesting chap that monk is."

Paul could not come to the next meeting, but he sent me a message: "I read the book. Very interesting. I wish there were medical certifications enclosed. By the way, I was born on the same day and month as Fr. Peter. Interesting!"

Dear Father Peter, I request that you unceasingly bless Paweł and all the prisoners, especially the participants of the prayer group meeting at the convict prisons.

We thank you, Father, for your ministry, faith, love, and generosity of your heart.

And, maybe, one more thing, a personal one. When I was taking Father and his retinue from the Jesuits' place for a common visit to the recidivists held at the prison in Bydgoszcz, Danusia [Fr. Peter's local assistant], asked by Fr. Peter, tied the strings of his shoes. It escaped from my mouth: "I'd like to do it as well" . . . To that, Father Superior [Jesuit] suggested: "all you need to do is untie the strings and then you'll be able to tie them up." Here I lacked the courage . . . and I regret it until today.

In the Lord, our God,

Anna Stranz and the ARKA Fellowship

Our Son Began to Wake Up From His Coma

On the day of August 31, 2004, my family was struck by a great tragedy. Our little 5-year-old daughter Kasia and 16-year-old Tom, our son Radek's friend, were killed instantly, while my wife Jolanta, Radek, and our other son—13-year-old Piotr (who remembers everything but refuses to talk about it)—were seriously injured in a car accident.

Radek sustained a severe trauma to his brainstem, had a broken jaw, a pierced lung, and many other injuries. He was in a state of coma for about 3 and a half months, and the doctors of our region did not give him any chances. However, we did not give up and believed all along that he would get out of that. After he was finally admitted to the Rehabilitation Clinic in Bydgoszcz, Radek slowly began to recover.

At the same time Fr. Peter Mary Rookey was visiting the clinic and prayed in person at Radek's bed. Thanks to our faith and the prayer, Radek began to wake up from his coma shortly after Fr. Peter's visit. At present, he is at home with all our family and we pray together full of hope and faith that Radek will fully recover. We have already lost so much.

Zbigniew Dzierzbicki

Giving Thanks

The December 2004 meeting with Fr. Peter in Bydgoszcz was, and continues to be, an unforgettable event for both me—a brother from the Congregation of the Holy Spirit, and tens of thousands of others—both religious and lay people. I thank God and the Blessed Virgin for that meeting many times. Now I wish to express this in writing.

Most Loving God! I thank you for having chosen a Servant so humble, engrossed in prayer, mortifying the flesh, and devoted to serving You Lord, Our Lady, and the people. May You be adored, oh Lord, for what I saw with my eyes at close range, for what happened within me and other souls over those couple of days, and which I will not manage to fully comprehend or express as a monk and a photographer.

Glory be to You, our Savior, for having touched me and my compatriots with Your Graces during Fr. Peter's ministry in two hospitals, three churches, chapels, cloisters, monastic communities, prison, and at Danusia's private home in Bydgoszcz only!

I humbly express my thanks for the celebrated Eucharists and prayer meetings, in which I took part and in which such crowds assembled that the hosts themselves, the Jesuit Fathers, did not remember have ever happened before. Thank you, Master, for the exceptional prayers, meditations and a sense of order emanating at every meeting. Eternal glory be to You, the Giver of Countless Gifts, for the returned hope thanks to Fr. Peter, for the faith that You are God acting yesterday, today, and forever by the power of the Sacraments of the Eucharist, and Priesthood, for the peace poured into my heart and the minds of so many people, for the burning love that yearns in us for "something more," for the enlivened faith in so many people getting closer to You, and for the gift of unity. Thanks be to You, the Redeemer, that it was not only You who were once laying your hands on those who were seeking Your help but also this modest monk who, in Your Name, was blessing, healing, and setting people free from their enslavements.

My gratitude and respect is to You for giving me and others the experience of Resting in the Holy Spirit, for the exceptional bliss, happiness, as well as the light coupled with the gift of peace, which settled within my own and other people's lives.

The Most Effective Redeemer, thank You also for the fruits of this priestly ministry and, especially, for the wonderful healing of Basia [a parishioner] who came to the Eucharist that was in thanksgiving for the visit of Fr. Peter. It was celebrated on January 29, 2005, at 7:00 PM, and Basia gave a witness testimony and showed that she could walk despite her many years' struggle with polio that had kept her wheelchair-bound and unable to walk on her own.

Glory be to You, Lord, for EVERYTHING.

With gratitude in my heart and memory at prayer,

Br. Hieronim Majka, CSSp

IV

FATHER PETER MARY ROOKEY, OSM, WITH THE PIARIST FATHERS IN WARSZAWA, ŁOWICZ, RZESZÓW, JASŁO, AND KRAKÓW

An Opportunity to Discover the Siekierki Sanctuary of Our Lady in Warszawa

The stay of Fr. Peter Mary Rookey, OSM, in the Sanctuary of Our Lady the Educatrix of the Youth, located at the Siekierki District of Warszawa, on December 13, 2004 marked a significant entry into the multiple procession of pilgrimages to this place chosen by Mary. Such pilgrimages began during the apparitions of Our Lady taking place there amid the raging evil of World War II, under the German occupation of the Polish land. When Warszawa was being destroyed, the people were persecuted, shot, taken away to prisons, and extermination or slave labor camps. Those who stayed in place, terrified and despairing inhabitants of Siekierki, gathered in the month of May at wayside crosses and little chapels and sang *the Litany of the Blessed Virgin Mary of Loreto.* In such circumstances, Mary appeared and passed words of encouragement and hope and an instruction to strengthen the faith and turn to Christ in full trust. The first apparition occurred on May 3, 1943, through the vision of a 12-year-old girl visionary named Wladzia. The apparitions lasted for over 6 years and helped the people live through the cruelty of the war. The apparitions ended with an appearance of Jesus giving an assurance that He would protect all those who would come back to Him.

Since the very beginning of those apparitions to Wladzia, people came to that place to strengthen their faith and obtain spiritual support and supernatural aid. Their number was steadily increasing as they expanded the little chapel built "among the ruins of destroyed Warszawa." The Primate of the Millennium, Servant of God, Cardinal Stefan Wyszynski instituted a pastoral center there, and he commended its custody to the Piarist Fathers. The next Primate of Poland, Cardinal Joseph Glemp, founded a parish consecrated to the Most Blessed Virgin Mary, the Queen of Confessors. Then, he raised its rank to a Sanctuary consecrated to Our Lady the Educatrix of the Youth. This holy place is visited by generations upon generations of Varsovians. Pilgrims from outside the capital city also go there. Pleas regarding various difficult problems flow out from there to God through the intercession of Mary, and abundant gifts flow down on the people in need. The people express gratefulness in the form of written thanks and thanksgiving votives. In one of her visions, Wladzia saw pearls scattered near Mary, representing the beads of the Rosary as well as the treasures of graces. That vision is being materialized now. People pray the Rosary here.

The decorations of the church interior are now dominated by a large white marble statue of Our Lady the Educatrix, standing under the large cross next to the tabernacle. In the evening of December 13, Fr. Peter Mary Rookey stood by Her, along with about 3000 pilgrims. The first of them came in as early as 3 hours before the scheduled communal Rosary, Mass, and prayer service at 5:30 PM. Apart from pilgrims from Warszawa and the surrounding region, there were organized guided groups arriving by motorcoaches from the distant cities of Bialystok, Siedlce, Minsk Mazowiecki among others . . . Those who came in earlier, said *the Chaplet to the Divine Mercy* (at 3:00 PM), sang songs, and visited the Sanctuary Chapel and the Chapel of Apparitions (located at the spot where the said apparitions actually took place). Many of the faithful endeavored to be as near to the altar in the church as possible. People stood in lines at the confessionals. Several priests were hearing confessions for about 4 hours. The crowds filling the church and the rear and side chorus galleries were seized by an atmosphere of praying, kindness, and expectation of a fulfillment of peoples' desires in the spirit of faith that there can be nothing impossible to God.

When Fr. Peter showed up, he was welcomed with an outburst of enthusiasm, which then waned into focused and ardent prayer. The sermon during the Holy Mass was interrupted several times by applause for Jesus for the successive cases of healing through Fr. Peter's prayers, about which he was giving testimonies. The congregated pilgrims—collectedly united with Christ in the Holy Communion despite the tightly filled-out space—continued to pray until 10:00 PM, singing songs to the tune of a spontaneously formed vocal and musical band and saying the Rosary with Fr. Eugeniusz, a Piarist, giving the meditations and intentions.

In such an enormous crowd of gathered pilgrims—for the most part weak, ill, aged and/or disabled—not a single person needed medical assistance. Also, the great physical stamina of Fr. Peter who prayed long and tirelessly over everyone and raised up his hand to bless EVERYONE with the sign of the Cross, was incomparably amazing! People were approaching him in long files, moving slowly up to the steps of the altar, all in good faith and hope. There were many who had the so-called Resting in the Holy Spirit. There was a woman who shouted out loud, trying to run away from the blessing, but the Power of God overcame the power of the evil manifestation. To move the people efficiently after the blessing, the Sacristy was opened, as well as the chapel and the corridors adjacent to the aisle of the church. They were directed to the passages for "rivers" of people—thoughtful, calmed, and delighted. They showed no trace of fatigue. Some of them, despite the difficulty, were finding a piece of the floor to stop, to kneel down or sit down on a little foldable chair, and to immediately concentrate on further praying. Others were returning to the emptied benches in the rear of the church to continue to focus on individual prayer, to meditate over what they were experiencing and, surely, to give thanks. The blessing by Fr. Peter ended just before 10:00 PM. There were also some persons who, individually, exchanged with Him a few words in the Sacristy.

Within a short time, it turned out that what was left after the visit and the prayers of Fr. Peter in the Sanctuary of Our Lady the Educatrix, were not only the nice memories, the book about him by Heather Parsons purchased by many, or the text of *The Miracle Prayer*, but also—above all—the spiritual fruits: deepened faith, spiritual strengthening, the experience of the healing work of Christ in the community of the Church. Probably the local Sanctuary had never held so many faithful gathered. For many who arrived for the meeting with Fr. Peter, it was also an opportunity to explore the Sanctuary as it was comparatively new and not widely known. The trouble was with many vehicles, for which there was not enough parking space at the Church parking lot and, because of that, a good part of them had to park in the lanes far away from the Sanctuary. Order-keepers worked very hard on that.

Praise be to Jesus and Mary for all that and, for Fr. Peter, here goes our traditional, Polish *May God reward you!*

Fr. Jan Taff, SP,
the Custodian of the Sanctuary

THE INCOMPREHENSIBLE—THE COMPREHENSIBLE

To Father Peter—my dear Friend, a Splendid Man and a Zealous Priest, I dedicate this

Jesus
Jesus from the Land of Nazareth
Distant and remote
Land of supreme feelings
Unfathomable and afflicted
Dawn of the rising sun
Invisible and apparent
Breath of the east wind
Gentle and permeating
Heart pulsating with love
Sanguine and glorious
Star radiating with hope
Old and new
Book of Divine Wisdom
Difficult and easy
Heaven of open hopes
Little and great
Brook of enlivening waters
Quiet and swift
Throne of the glorious majesty
Humble and triumphant
Jesus . . .
Buried and Alive
I Love You . . .

If one wanted to characterize the phenomenon of Fr. Peter Rookey's life by the use of a concise definition, one might propose an expression, "incomprehensible-comprehensible." The dialectics of this expression comprises the life of the priest who follows the Master of Nazareth. On his way of faithfully imitating Jesus, he experiences—on the one hand—his being misunderstood and rejected and—on the other hand—his being understood and accepted.

On the last visit of Fr. Peter to Poland I had an opportunity to meet with him at the Piarist Fathers' Sanctuary of Our Lady the Educatrix of the Youth on December 13, 2004. As I lectured in Lublin [at the local Catholic university] into late hours in that afternoon, I could reach Warsaw only in the evening. Fr. Peter greeted me with jubilation, and we had an opportunity to converse together until the late night hours. Despite an exhaustingly busy schedule, Fr. Peter did not show any fatigue. In a special way, we were reminiscing about the time of our joint pilgrimage to the Holy Land in April 2004.

Our way through Jerusalem, Bethlehem, Capharnaum, the Mount of Tabor, the Mount of the Beatitudes, and Nazareth brought us near to each other and allowed us to experience the gift of our priesthood with great intensity. Looking at Fr. Peter, I learned from him how to combine an intensive and profound prayer with involvement for the benefit of persons met on our way. In particular, what stuck in my memory was our stay at the Home of Peace—an orphanage on the Mount of Olives—where Fr. Peter prayed and blessed all the children and the Sisters with great paternal devotion. I saw the children's faces beam with joy and hope for a better tomorrow.

All along our pilgrimage, Fr. Peter bestowed a similar respect and warmth upon the Arabs, Jews, and Christians. I learned from him that love and prayer for the neighbor should not be limited by the ethnical and religious criteria but that every man should be at the center of priestly influence. Fr. Peter possesses this special charism of being a good listener and a sensitive receiver. He often manually accommodates his own hearing aid to make it easier for him to listen more intently to the words of his interlocutors. However, he has a yet another sense of seeing through a person with his deep look and listening to him or her not just with his ears but also with his whole heart. Sometimes Father seemed to be faraway, as if closed within his own world but, whenever somebody started a conversation with him, that person would find out straight off that Father "seized" the issue quickly and permeated it with his mind strictly consistent with Jesus' way. During the concelebrated Holy Mass, I saw Fr. Peter pray fervently and attach to the sacrifice of Jesus all the daily matters. The Eucharist constitutes for him the center of life and the driving force of fruitful activity. So many people were coming to Father, asking for a blessing and a healing prayer. I saw the zeal and total involvement with which Father was answering their requests and reading the desires of their hearts.

I am glad that I could meet such a priest in my own lifetime. When I was saying goodbye to Father in Warszawa, it was already after 1:00 AM. Father was still joking and was in the prime of his life. He talked about the intensive program planned for him for the days to follow. I thought to myself then—how many charisms a man receives from God when he answers willingly to His calling and fulfills His mission with total devotion. Looking intently with great love into the figure of the Holy Mother of God, Fr. Peter—in his humility, trust, and fervent prayer—answers to God every day: "Yes, my Lord, here I am, do send me."

Fr. Mirosław Stanisław Wróbel, PhD,
a Catholic University Professor

FROM THE HOLY LAND TO POLAND AND . . . BACK TO POLAND

The meeting with Fr. Peter belongs to history now, but the memories are still alive and, by saying *The Miracle Prayer*, we are all the time together before the Lord. This highly amazing unity, heartiness and confidence could be felt ever since the first meeting with Fr. Peter, when he, along with a group of pilgrims, made a stopover in Warszawa for a prayer group on their way back from the Holy Land in April 2004.

Never before had I heard about this priest. Several days before Easter 2004, my friend called me and gave me some fascinating information about a "monk who heals." She concluded our conversation by reading *The Miracle Prayer*. All that sounded very reliable—a priest who healed by the power of Lord Jesus, Who himself was healed miraculously many years ago, and—by way of thanks—offered up his own life for the sole service to the Lord; in addition, he is a great devotee of the Queen of Peace.

The desire to attend the meeting was predominant during the days that followed, and the organizational effort supported by prayer brought about the awaited result. Among the pilgrims, there was a priest, Fr. Peter, in plain black clothing with a gigantic cross embroidered on the back of his jacket and a smaller one on the left front part of his jacket—on his heart. The man was of the dignified age, full of joy, peace, warmth, and cordiality. He was radiating with kindness. He was constantly making surprises by showing concern for others, by making amiable gestures of help, by showing gratitude for a merest trifle, by his bravado (he outpaced me on the stairs by taking 2-step leaps on going upward to hold the door for me, so I could enter first), and by his great sense of humor. Everything was so spontaneous and joyful!

The most important part of the meeting was the Eucharist and, afterward, an individual blessing during which some of the persons experienced Resting in the Holy Spirit. I looked with admiration on the face beaming with God's love and peace. He was giving back every spare moment to Mary. As a Good Shepherd, with a rosary in his hand, he went around our group preoccupied with their travel baggage. He himself was making an impression of being detached from that "reality" of ours—he seemed to be united with Jesus and Mary, whispering Hail-Mary decades.

*   *   *

In December 2004, Fr. Peter came on an official pilgrimage to Poland. Among the many cities on his route, he also visited Warszawa and, there, he had one great meeting with the faithful at the Sanctuary of Our Lady the Educatrix of the Youth at the Siekierki district of Warszawa. As it was later proved, that prayer meeting was the most numerously attended of all the celebrations ever having been held in that church. Fr. Peter delivered a sermon. It was a joyful witness to the wonders of Divine Providence made real through his mediation. The witnesses were interspersed with cries of "Halleluiah" and ovations for Jesus. Those words boosted the faith and hope of the gathered people; some of them received the gift of tears. The confessionals were besieged for over 4 hours. After the end of the Holy Mass, *The Miracle Prayer* was said before the Cross and the individual blessings began, starting with the priests and the altar boys and, afterward, all the faithful gathered. The thirsty congregation stood up in lines before the altar, and Fr. Peter moved glibly from the left to the right and back in order not to skip anybody. There was hope, admiration, and awe visible on the faces of the expectant people, and Fr. Peter was standing with the Cross in his hand before every person individually, taking a brief look at each person coming up, which was also a "meeting"—an internal communion in complete understanding and love.

The Lord was, indeed, working through his hands. When his hand, wielding the Cross, rose up to the level of my eyes, my physical power receded and I was softly laid to rest on the church floor. My heart was pounding as if it wanted to fly away, my will was utterly subjected to God's Will and stayed so for a long time after I rose to my feet from the rest, and there was peace, joy, and silence dwelling in me.

Fr. Peter unremittingly and self-sacrificingly wished to meet everyone individually; to bless and delight each and everyone with the enthusiasm of his faith. After Fr. Peter left, a lot of people continued to pray despite the late hours.

*   *   *

To the jubilation of the severely sick persons, Fr. Peter also came to one of the Varsovian hospitals. With his words of comfort, he brought the gift of strengthening faith and hope; trust and blessing. He made a mention of the gift of scent that can appear during prayer. With concern, he was bestowing gifts upon all the people with whom he encountered in the chapel, in the elevator, on the stairs, or in the ICU room. He had time for conversation and reflection. Having seen the portrait of St. Padre Pio, he reminisced that he had met him, went to him for a confession, and that St. Padre Pio had the gift of permeating the human conscience.

Sometimes the Lord puts on our way persons who are exceptional and gifted with special graces. Such meetings become imprinted as a pattern into our hearts forever. Just like Fr. Peter was still cherishing very vivid memories of St. Padre Pio—the saint whom I consider nearest to my heart—I will be forever thankful for the gift of the meeting, the communal prayer, and God's blessing. Looking at his works from aside, I would like to have said, "have a rest a little, good Father, for you are tired." But no—he would go on, because yet another congregation was waiting for him in yet another city.

*   *   *

The last part of his visit was in Kraków. It turned out that our Guest had gotten ill on the second day (Sunday) of his stay in that city. He did not deliver a sermon. He came up to the altar to give out a general blessing with the Holy Sacrament in a roundabout procession through the church aisles. In fact, he gently pushed his way through the crowd, advancing from all sides to touch even a piece of his monk's habit. Pale, tired, sweating, but continually smiling and with his light look, Fr. Peter was plying forward behind Jesus in the Monstrance, protected a little by his friends. It was evident he wished to look at everyone, to meet with each person individually. At times, he made a stop and touched those standing nearest him. After returning to the altar, he sang the prayer with a hoarse voice and blessed the crowded congregation with great esteem and reverence. It was a most tremendous experience for me. The priest who, several days before, served 4000 people all in one church only, here—apparently exhausted and weak . . . but continuing his duty!

Fr. Peter always repeats, "it is the Lord Jesus who heals; He Himself chooses the time, the place, and the kind of grace that are the most necessary to the salvation of a particular man."

St. Padre Pio wrote: *Do not reject the cross that the Heavenly Father gives you, because He does this to liken you to His own Son of God. Never run into depression in face of all the new crosses that Heaven bestows upon you, because such is just the fate of all the people who have chosen Crucified Jesus as their own little part. Persevere at prayer and at good reading. In practicing all this, always have in your mind only the glory of God and your pleasing Him* (*Padre Pio's Letters.* The correspondence with Mrs. Rafaelina Cerase, Pietrelcina, 04. 25. 1914)

Grateful Danuta

DOES OUR LORD REALLY WANT ME TO OPEN UP TO RECEIVE THIS GIFT?

Our Lord told us to go to cities and hamlets in order to heal the sick and proclaim
that the Kingdom of God was near . . . so I believe that all priests are called,
to a smaller or greater degree, to the healing ministry in the name of Jesus.
(Fr. Peter Mary, a quote from *Man of Miracles*, pp 27-28)

I am a chaplain in the hospital, where Fr. Peter prayed over the sick during his stay in Warszawa. His visit was unexpected and surprising to me. The organizers of Father's visit to Poland did not warrant that it would come about for sure. But it did, and I am happy because of that.

First of all, I met a priest involved with Medjugorje. I have lived Our Lady's messages for over 20 years, and they have caused me to change from being a doctor to being a priest; from a man praying little to a priest who spends many hours adoring the Lord Jesus in the Holy Sacrament.

Second, the sick persons were surely comforted and received graces, and the meeting itself was very fruitful.

Third, there were some cases of certain recovery from disease, although I was not given any written testimonies about it.

Fourth, I myself give out the Sacrament of the Anointing of the Sick and I pray over the patients every week. By some strange event, already in 2004, I was asked three times by different persons to pray for healing of the sick. The last time it happened after I had returned from Medjugorje. I went to confession. My confessor, a priest unknown to me, told me to lay my hands on the sick and ask God for their healing by the Power of Jesus (I thought to myself, "How did this idea come to his mind?"). And, indeed, I did anoint a sick person one day before Fr. Peter's arrival. On the day of Father's visit, while passing through the ward in the evening, I heard that the condition of that sick person had improved; the patients sharing the same hospital room with her said that it had happened after I had anointed her.

One day after Father's visit, which was Wednesday, I celebrated a Holy Mass for the intention of the recovery of another sick person. Then, one week later, her mother came to me and said that, on the day on which I had celebrated the Holy Mass, the cancer her daughter had suffered from disappeared—it did not show up during follow-up medical testing. They ascribe that to the celebrated Holy Mass also. Yet, there was another (the third) person whose condition also improved and it was considered an effect of the unction, too.

However, I did not know whether the Lord indeed wanted me to open up to this gift, and Father's visit was a great help for me in this regard; but time is needed to prove it or not.

Fifth, my own allergy problems diminished after Father's visit, and although they have not disappeared completely, I—at least—could stop taking medications.

Surely, this was an edifying time for me and the Holy Spirit was leading me as a priest to an enlivening of my faith.

Fr. Maciej, a Chaplain

AN AMBASSADOR OF JESUS AND MARY TO POLAND

An impression that it was "one big dream" has not left me until today—it refers to the Pilgrimage to the Holy Land during the Holy Week of 2004. A group of pilgrims from different areas, mostly of Poland, but also of the world (Lithuania and the USA)—the individuals for the most part unknown to each other—became a Joyful Fellowship thanks to the very unusual "radiance" of Fr. Peter Mary Rookey's peacefulness, humor, humble prayer, and servant-like and fully discreet concern about everyone.

His majestic figure attracted my attention at the PKP Railroad Station in Krakow, Poland, from where we were to go by train to Warszawa and, afterward, take a flight from the Okęcie Airport to Tel Aviv, Israel, then farther on (by bus) to JERUSHALAIM—the City of Peace.

My first thought was that this hoary man in a black jacket with the Jerusalem Cross emblazoned on it was accompanying his relatives who were to take the train . . . . As it proved to be, he was a co-participant of our pilgrimage. While on the train, I found out that he was an American priest who had arrived by plane in Poland to share the Way to the Holy Land along with us.

We were carrying a little statue of Our Lady of Medjugorje, the Queen of Peace with us, which was to be given to the Franciscans at the Basilica of the Holy Sepulchre in Jerusalem. Mary embodied in that statue wandered with us on Palm Sunday—downhill from the Mount of Olives. In my memory, I keep the joy of Fr. Peter's, when it was his turn to carry Her in his arms during the procession. I found out about his great devotion to Our Lady from the book *Man of Miracles*. (I encourage the publisher to renew the edition of this book, so that as many people as possible may learn about Fr. Peter's charism.)

After reading that book in the Holy Land, I found out that many persons had experienced the gift of Resting in the Holy Spirit following Fr. Peter's prayer and blessing of them. I was skeptically disposed to that; I was not in a position to believe in that until I myself experienced such a grace several times during the pilgrimage and, after returning to Poland, at the Jesuits' church in Warszawa, where there are the relics of St. Andrew Bobola.

And here, in December 2004, I meet with Fr. Peter once more—again in Warszawa; this time in the Siekierki district, in the Sanctuary of Our Lady the Educatrix of the Youths, where the hosts were the Piarist Fathers.

How shall I express my impressions from this meeting in a few statements?

The fact that I had arrived at the Sanctuary on time, coming all the way from distant Kolobrzeg, was thanks to an unknown Varsovian taxi driver who piloted me through Warszawa, a city, with which I was completely unfamiliar. I already could think of it as of a "little miracle." Once I came close to the Sanctuary and saw the enormous crowds of the faithful, I felt that surely an uncommon event was about to happen . . . . a heartfelt welcome by Fr. Peter in the Sacristy became a reward for the effort of traveling. The Father's homily (splendidly interpreted) during the Eucharist well deserves to be a pattern to imitate. It won my heart that Father turned the attention of all the participants of the meeting to Jesus in the Eucharist and the Presence of Mary who is always where Her Son is.

Certainly, Siekierki had not experienced such devotion previously, but I think that it was that "very strange" decree of the Divine Providence that brought Our Lady's devotees to the Place, where She had come down from Heaven. Many of us present there learned about the Varsovian Apparitions of the Virgin Mary at Siekierki just then. To make it known to those unfamiliar with meaningfulness of that place, Mary used Her own priest from the US to deliver to us the power of Jesus and the Love of the Immaculate Virgin Mary and attract so many people to that event.

Grateful for the gift of meeting with Fr. Peter at the Altar of Jesus, with my priestly prayer, blessing, and wishes of staying under Mary's Protection,

Fr. Zdzisław Grochal

First in Jerusalem, Then in Warszawa

I learned about Father Peter Mary Rookey thanks to having read the Polish version of the book titled *Man of Miracles*. I was fascinated by the content of that publication showing him to be humble and obedient to the guidance of the Divine Providence. I was also edified by the many witnesses of persons who, in simple words, showed the world God's work when their life experience exceeded the human ability to withstand harsh suffering.

I want, however, to admit sincerely that I was not always in a position to believe in every bit of what the witnesses of those selected persons who experienced a miracle of spiritual or even physical healing were saying. As they affirmed, they had received such graces as a result of a priestly blessing by the power of God through Fr. Peter, having been gifted with the grace of the healing charism. Such is our human imperfection that, in our life, we have to, all the time, seek an extra confirmation of what God gives us for free, in His own infinite love touching us, but we are unable to accept it, because we . . . have our ears but we do not hear; we have our eyes but we do not see.

I met Fr. Peter in person in the Holy Land in April 2004, when I was working there, voluntarily serving handicapped and disabled children. One day, I joined a Polish group of pilgrims on their visit to the place of the Nativity in Bethlehem. I got on the bus and, right off, there came a surprise. How overjoyed I was when I recognized God's priest from distant America among the befriended Poles.

Fr. Peter at once made a very favorable impression on me. A medium-size, elderly man with a nice and joyful disposition, obliging, independent, deeply focused on sacred matters, always ready to help every person.

Only later did I understand that God had had a plan in that I met him right there—on the Land of Jesus, to understand many things better and, at the same time, to recognize the working of God in our lives, which we do not live by chance. I was soon to find out for sure that Fr. Peter, the servant of God, came to the Holy Land because God wanted so.

It turned out later that he had been needed here to use the power of God in special circumstances to obtain, by his humble prayer, the gift of healing for a person whom God had invited to a great, humanly inexplicable, suffering.

Two days prior to our surely not accidental meeting with Fr. Peter, I found out about Fr. Anthony suddenly becoming seriously ill. Father Anthony was a young Franciscan priest fulfilling his mission at the Holy Sepulchre in Jerusalem. I was told that Fr. Anthony was unconscious and had been taken to an Israeli hospital and that his condition was hopeless. Father Anthony happened to be in the Judean Desert, where—for no apparent reason—he fainted suddenly; it soon turned out that almost all his organs, except for his brain, had stopped functioning.

I remembered then that I had with me *The Miracle Prayer* authored by Fr. Peter. He was used to using that prayer as an introductory prayer to blessing the faithful. I had earlier rewritten it from the already mentioned book. I took it with me on my trip to the Holy Land, not knowing then why. I now understand that it was under God's "control." I said the prayer, hoping that by those entreaties a miracle would take place for Fr. Anthony in this hopeless situation. As if in reply to my trust, 2 days later, God put on my way this servant of God—the priest from the USA, who had come to the land of Jesus, just at *that* time.

As soon as he heard about the critical, almost irreversible condition of his priestly brother (Fr. Anthony), Fr. Peter started to "bombard" Heaven. He supported us with his own prayer, sending the suffering priest his blessing spiritually, since he could not do it (to pray over Fr. Anthony) in person; the priest whom only God could help because human efforts already proved ineffective. All the human calculations and reasoning failed here, for only an intervention by God could have any effect, because the doctors did not see a chance for Fr. Anthony's recovery.

And it was just such a miraculous help from Heaven that we obtained for Fr. Anthony by sincerely and fervently saying *The Miracle Prayer*. Fr. Peter contributed to this miraculous healing in a special way, just by being *there* and praying at *that time*.

After a month of staying in a critical condition, Fr. Anthony inexplicably began to recover his physical fitness and, so to speak, came back "from the other world." And, after 6 months, he recuperated from his gravely serious condition almost entirely and was able to work normally and go on fulfilling his mission at the Holy Sepulchre in Jerusalem. He now serves there affectionately and with great gratitude. That was humanly inexplicable but, for God, everything is possible.

Medical records of the entire course of Fr. Anthony's case and his inexplicable healing can be obtained from him. Giving thanks to God for the miracle of his healing, he also wishes to thank all the people for their prayers and Fr. Peter for his intercessional prayers and spiritual blessing.

That was in the Holy Land [in April 2004].

*   *   *

In December 2004, I heard that Fr. Peter Mary Rookey, OSM, permanently living in the USA, was to come to Poland. I also learned that he would be in Warszawa on December 13, where there would be a special prayer service held along with Fr. Peter's priestly blessing.

I desired to take part in that service not only for myself but I also felt an immense need for organizing a pilgrimage for many persons needing such prayer and the ministry of Father. At the beginning, I absolutely did not know how to go about informing and encouraging persons who were interested in such a meeting. I knew that it was an exceptional opportunity to help many people to have a chance to meet with God through the prayer and the charismatic ministry of the priest who, by living out the love of God day by day, carries Jesus with all of his own personality; who, by serving every person in need, opens up the hearts of all people to the gifts of God's Mercy.

I prayed for this intention and considered how to do it. God heard me and came to my aid by putting the right people on my way. I talked to my daughter who had earlier read the book and also desired to meet Fr. Peter and pray together with him. We spoke of the possible meeting with many persons whom we knew, extending the circle of the interested persons this way. We were lending the book for reading and making the person of Father and the gift of his ministry closer to them this way. All that was not enough, however, because few persons were open to this special action of God. After some time, we were given an opportunity to broadcast this issue and inform the faithful on a wider scale over the Podlasie regional Catholic radio. I participated in one broadcast and had but a few minutes to present the whole matter. That was enough time to shortly characterize the charism of Fr. Peter and the grace of God's work in his life. I dreamt to encourage at least a handful of people to go to the meeting, whereas the number of people who participated was big enough to occupy six buses. So this is how God works!

The meeting took place in a large church of Our Lady the Educatrix of the Youth, at the Siekierki District of Warszawa. The large, modern church, with a capacity allowing space for several-thousand people, was densely crowded. Many diseased persons, crippled, handicapped, wheelchair-bound, and mothers holding little children in their arms came to the church, just like in the times of Jesus, when He was walking and preaching, and followed by the crowds of crippled, blind, and demon-possessed people.

The long meeting lasting hours began with the Rosary, then a Holy Mass was celebrated to the accompaniment of a band singing songs to the Holy Spirit and other songs. During the Holy Mass, Fr. Peter delivered a homily in English, which was interpreted to Polish to make it understood and properly received by all the faithful. No sooner than he was done with his sermon and had made his own priest-style show, Fr. Peter had ignited the hearts of everyone present with immense hope and joy. Smiles beamed on many faces. Others who came to the Mass were now oblivious to their pain.

As soon as the Holy Mass had ended and the prayer meeting led by Father was begun in preparation to receive God's blessing, everyone was much focused, yet joyful with hope. A large Cross and the lights were placed on the main altar. Barbara, who accompanied Father, greatly concentrated, read out loud *The Miracle Prayer*, which was repeated by the faithful. After a while, Fr. Peter started to bless the faithful and put the sign of a spiritual Cross on their foreheads, using the Cross containing the relics of the Servite saints. He blessed each person individually, carrying Jesus to all the distressed and love-deprived hearts.

In the first instance, he blessed the priests who were kneeling down with humility, and in this way set an example for us all to follow. Next, the gathered faithful came to the altar, maintaining a due order all the time, despite the crowdedness. Sometimes, it happened that someone who was impatient or who was enduring more suffering pushed his way to receive the blessing earlier than the others but, there too, the faithful were greatly understanding, which permitted everyone to approach Father in due time. Many persons received the grace of Resting in the Holy Spirit during the blessing.

At a certain moment, a terrifying scream resounded in the church, which aroused a kind of alarm and some confusion. Many persons present did not know what to do. It was probably a person whose heart was somehow troubled by an activity of an evil spirit, and this was why there was such a loud reaction to the blessing by the power of Jesus. Father Peter stopped for a moment by that person to give her a special blessing. As the horrible loud, guttural sounds were still coming from deep within her, she was encircled by a group of praying faithful and priests providing special support. I believe that God Himself allowed such a situation to occur to make everyone aware that evil really exists, and to see that the real Presence of Jesus among us overcomes evil by His blessings through priestly hands. He comes to us through the ministry of this chosen, humble priest who came to us from far across the ocean to say to us that Jesus is alive and present among us, by working miracles, healing, revealing His presence, and casting out demons, but we must have faith in Him.

After that special meeting with Jesus revealing Himself in signs so necessary for us to believe in God and love Him with all our hearts, many persons opened up to the work of God—each one in a different way. I received many telephone calls and personal thanks for the possibility of meeting Fr. Peter who gave witness of his limitless trust in God and Mary by blessing us and bringing us closer to Jesus.

The gift of prayer as well as the special blessing and ministry of Fr. Peter contributed to the fact that many persons felt the extraordinary working of Divine

Mercy through physical or spiritual healing. May some of their testimonies provide evidence that Jesus came to their weary lives and made a miracle so that they may believe.

*   *   *

My testimony: The trip to Warszawa for the prayer meeting with Fr. Peter on the day of December 13, 2004, was a tremendous experience. I was very happy that I could once again meet with this man of God through whom Jesus entered my life. I was also glad that I had succeeded in organizing such a large group of people who desired to take part in such a meeting. My two daughters also went along with me: Dorota who has been seeking God all the time in her own young life, and Renata concerned about deepening her own love for Jesus so she can give it to others. She helped me in organizing the trip, but when the time came, she found it hard to go with us. At the last moment, literally, she managed to overcome all the difficulties and joined the elect group happily. Satan was not on vacation and was doing everything to annihilate our plans and intentions. He tried to exact vengeance on me, too, but God took over the control.

Just before our trip, I found out that my son had had a car accident. At that moment, however, I was as if "thunderstruck" leaving the matter of the accident to God, I gave myself up completely to the pilgrims whom I wished to bring to achieve the goal. Only the next day did I realize how much I was subjected to a test of trusting God to serve the people.

The car accident in which my son was involved looked very bad. God, however, brought some good out of it. Here is how it happened. My son was passing another car and, suddenly, lost his grip of the steering wheel. His car rolled over into a deep ditch, and somersaulted, turning over several times until it finally landed on its roof. The car was totaled completely, but my son came out of the accident **without (!)** a broken bone or even a scratch on his body. The material loss was huge as it was a brand new car, but my son lives on and feels fine, and works normally. As it turned out, the result of this attempt of exacting vengeance by Satan had a blessed effect, because the whole situation contributed to my son becoming even closer to God.

One can read this as a sign of Satan's vengeance for my relentless efforts to make it possible for a great group of people to come to a meeting with Jesus. Jesus was present in a special way through the ministry of Fr. Peter who, coming to us from the USA, carried God to us within his heart differently—through his example of humility and fervent faith.

My daughter who sought God on her own, also found joy and peace there. Until then she believed that God existed but could not overcome a feeling of anxiety that unceasingly paralyzed her internally and tormented her life. Now she has regained her peace of mind and—as she has said—she understands that

God had another way for her to follow. Nowadays, she is able to accept God's Will without any reservation in every situation that God has designed for her. She calmly resolves all the difficulties and problems piling up in her life without any unnecessary excitement. I notice now my daughter behaves with great prudence (proof of God's action) and undertakes appropriate and right decisions despite her young age.

I thank God for all these various experiences and happenings that helped me find more love, more joy, and internal peace in both my personal and family life.

Glory to the Lord!

Helena Sosnowska

I Decided to Support That Priest's Ministry With My Prayer

After a check-up USG scanning of my breast, I was told that I was seriously ill. The doctor who was doing the long examination announced that she was obliged to tell me that a large change was visible in the anatomical structure of my breast. At the same time, she recommended that I see an oncologist at once. I could not delay even a day because it was so serious and urgent. The medical diagnosis was a shock to me—as if I had heard a death sentence.

After having learned about my disease, I experienced variable moods—moments of despair and weeping, then, sometimes, a strange joy—as if I were at ease with my disease. There were even such moments when I was happy—as if I were not ill at all. During this difficult time, I was supported by two persons who cheered me up by repeatedly saying, "everything will be fine, you will see."

I did not speculate about how that would be; I trusted God completely instead; I trusted Him all the way by accepting everything that might possibly happen to me.

I heard about Fr. Peter's visit to Poland, and I signed up for a trip to Warszawa for a common Eucharist with a healing prayer.

I went to the Mass and healing service receptive to anything that might happen. I believed that it would be the way God wanted it to be. If I were to leave this world, it meant that it had to be so, not otherwise. I was completely reconciled with that, and I repeated all the time, "**Jesus, I trust in Thee,**" and, **"Thy Will be done."** I did not think for a moment, as I was going to the vigil, that God would heal me. I did not concentrate on myself but decided to support the priest's ministry with my prayer—such was my yearning. So, on that day, I only prayed and fasted for the intentions of Fr. Peter and his ministry.

Once we got inside the church of Our Lady the Educatrix of the Youth, in Warszawa, I prayed very fervently during the meditation of the mysteries of the Holy Rosary that preceded the Eucharist. At a certain moment, I felt enormous heat—it started at my head and passed down to my chest.

When the Holy Mass began, Fr. Peter explained in his homily that there was a St. Peregrine who is a patron of those who are struck by cancer and that, through his intercession, we can ask for a grace of healing from cancer. After hearing these words, I immediately rested in the Holy Spirit. Prior to that time, I had experienced the grace of Resting in the Holy Spirit on several occasions, but never as a result of my listening to words. At the time of experiencing the rest, I had something like a movie reel playing in front of my eyes, in which I saw one by one persons who had mistreated me and whom I had never forgiven.

In the Name of Jesus, I repeated all the time, "**Jesus I trust in Thee,**" and "**Thy Will be done, my Lord.**"

The words of *The Miracle Prayer*, uttered after the end of the Holy Mass, were heard by me for the first time. They were a confirmation that what I had heard and experienced earlier was by the work of God.

Further on, God so arranged everything that, during the prayer vigil in Warszawa, I felt that I was healed. After returning home, the next day, I visited the doctor. She told me that I was completely healthy, had no tumor anymore, and that there were no signs of the disease. Repeated USG scanning and mammography confirmed her findings. The doctor who did the tests said that he did not see any disease. He asked how it had happened that the disease that was visible earlier on the scan was then no longer there. I answered that I had been healed. To the doctor's remark, "I guess you've probably been to some healer," I answered, "**Yes, I was, but not to "some," but the Only Healer—Jesus Christ.**"

All I experienced has permitted me lately to understand that I need to evermore serve God and His people—who are the Church. I must help others by praying for the graces for those people who need them, help out with all my soul those who are called to serve, and talk about what I have experienced. By granting me the grace of a miraculous healing, God reminded me once more about my assignment, clearly showing me what I am to do.

Thanks be to God!

Krystyna

I Was Happy I Could Pray Among Those Who Had Devoted Themselves to Jesus and Mary

A dozen or so years ago, I became ill and it was caused by my ear labyrinth impairment. It is a complex disease and very troublesome in everyday life. I was constantly dizzy and had headaches; the whole room would spin; my body couldn't keep balance. After visiting my doctor and taking the prescribed medications, I noticed a partial recession of my disease, but it was recurring and it was painful. I could only sleep on my left side, because, every change of position and every attempt to settle myself on the other side or on my back caused a strong headache and dizziness immediately. Recently, I was feeling a sensation of spinning in my head and would lose my balance while even going down the street. I could not sleep and was afraid to go outside by myself, because the vertigo and lack of coordination of my body movements made it impossible to lead a normal life.

In October 2004, I saw a laryngologist and he referred me for a special treatment. I underwent the treatment but, unfortunately, after a month, I felt even worse. My hands were trembling—from the palms to the elbows, and my legs—from the hips to the knees. I had no strength to move or do anything. I felt as if I had gotten up from bed after some serious illness. I was unable to carry a glass of tea from the kitchen to another room.

I knew what the disease of the labyrinth of the ear meant and its possible outcome. I was afraid that I would soon be unable to move on my own. I entrusted all my concerns to Jesus, however, and thought that even if I am to suffer so much, I will then offer it all for the conversion of sinners. I only asked the Lord God that He would not leave me alone but would help me in this suffering through His Mercy. I kept telling Him, "Thy will be done."

In December 2004, I found out about a meeting with Fr. Peter to be held in Warszawa. I signed up for the Eucharistic meeting including the "Miracle Prayer." My desire was to worship God at that prayer vigil and ask Him to heal my spirit and to convert my family. I was very happy that I could participate in that special meeting and pray among those who had surrendered themselves to Jesus and Mary.

After a Rosary prayer and the Eucharist, *The Miracle Prayer* was said and, then, Fr. Peter blessed everyone with the Cross with relics held in his hand. I also approached him to receive the individual blessing of Jesus through the hand of His priest—Fr. Peter. During the blessing, I experienced the grace of Resting in the Holy Spirit. I was laid down on my back, and I felt a severe headache, characteristic of the labyrinth disease, but without the giddiness. Many times had I experienced the grace of Resting in the Holy Spirit but, at that time, it lasted for a very long time as did the headache. After some time, I managed to sit up and a priest with an altar boy took me to the Sacristy. Once there, I continued to feel some weakness in my legs but no longer did I have the trembling of my hands. I felt thirsty for very cold water, and I drank a whole glass of it. Some time later, I went with my friend to pray, because Fr. Peter was still blessing. When the meeting finished, I returned home, and I felt magnificent. My hands were not trembling, I was full of joy, love, and peace. When I laid down to sleep, a thought came up, "Try to lay on your right side." So I did it slowly and did not feel any dizziness or headache; I lied down on my back; I turned over—and it was easy; there was no pain. Also, neither my hands nor legs trembled. Only then did I realize that I had been healed, so I began to adore God for the miracle of my healing with all my heart.

Until now, I have no complaints. I can work normally. I am very happy, full of joy, love, and thankfulness to God and people. These feelings overfill me. Herein, I wish to thank God and Fr. Peter and all the people who contributed to my physical cure. It has made me love God even more with all my trust and affection.

Jesus is still among us; He teaches, heals, and works miracles. We only have to believe and trust in Him with the fullness of love.

Thanks be to God!

Alina

The People Kept Coming and Coming and Coming . . .

I had not read any book about Fr. Peter before meeting with him. I did not read any book after the meeting. I spent only several hours in his proximity—so what can I write about him?

As a 27-year-old priest, I was impressed by his vitality. Here he is, an 88-year-old man who had come to our church in Lowicz after Warszawa. On the preceding day, he had served people at church until late into the night and here another long evening was about to start. Despite his self-apparent fatigue, Fr. Peter joked, spoke with us, and found the time to give an interview. His failing hearing aid was adding some trouble—a squeaking sound was audible even to the persons standing by, let alone to himself. Fr. Peter, however, did not utter a single word of complaint. And when the Eucharist began, Father was reinvigorated. After the Holy Mass, he gave individual blessings. People kept coming and coming and coming . . . while Fr. Peter was putting the sign of the Cross on their foreheads with great love and joy. Sometimes he patted someone on the shoulder, sometimes he gently stroked the person's cheek. He was completely unconcerned whether there were still 100, 500, 1000, or 5000 more still waiting—he was available for everyone at a given moment until he was done with the last person. Afterward he bent with his faith and love over three demon-possessed persons to request their liberation through his fervent prayers.

Where do such energy and power come from? Where does such love for man come from? No doubt, from Jesus. When I looked at Fr. Peter that evening, a statement from St Paul's Letter to the Galatians (Gal 2:20) came to my mind, *Yet I live, no longer I, but Christ lives in me; insofar as I now live in the flesh, I live by faith in the Son of God who has loved me and given himself up for me.* Father Peter truly surrendered his life, all of himself, to Jesus. Without enumerating his merits, without saving anything, without retaining anything for himself, he allowed Jesus to freely make use of him.

How much would I like to be able to do the same . . .

Fr. Marek Kudach, SP

Fr. Peter's Obedience Spoke to Me Volumes More Than What He Had Done Before

Ever since the first moment when I found out that Fr. Peter Mary Rookey, OSM, was coming to Poland from the USA to offer his intercessional prayers, I felt an internal pressure to go to the meeting. Never before had I heard about Fr. Peter, yet the short information on his life and priestly ministry, which I read in the monthly *Znak Pokoju* [*The Sign of Peace*] made him someone very close to me from the start, someone trustworthy and bringing life to one's hope in God.

I was moved most of all by his test of obedience, to which he had withstood for 33 years. To stop his ministry of intercessional prayer full of God's blessing and Divine fruits, to stop it when its application was in great demand from "those who are unwell"—can be humanly viewed as absolutely unwise and a waste of God-given talents. In the human thinking, some questions need to be raised: "Is it necessary? Would it not be better to continue the ministry without being obedient, to be driven by good intention and earthly judgment? After all, the Lord is with me, because He has restored my eyesight and blesses my priestly ministry!" So . . . "Padre Pio, what would you advise me to do in this situation?"—Fr. Peter asked. "Father Peter, be obedient to Jesus present in His Church"—was Padre Pio's answer. Be obedient in a kindhearted way to the end, without trying to use human diplomacy. Be the grain that, thrown into the ground of obedience and humility, will decay there completely to bring about a still more abundant crop.

Fr. Peter's mother had obtained for him by her prayers not only a miraculous restoration of his physical eyesight but also a grace of deep faith that allowed him to entrust his own life to God and His Wisdom. The 33 years of his life in obedience to Christ is a great secret of his faith, by which Fr. Peter proclaimed the death of Christ and confessed His Resurrection. *For to me life is Christ* (Phil 1:21), who was crucified with obedience and humility unto His death, *yet I live, no longer I, but Christ lives in me; insofar as I now live in the flesh, I live by faith in the Son of God who has loved me and given himself up for me* (Gal 2:20)—Fr. Peter can say after St. Paul. In his dying on the cross of obedience, God's love ripened in the priestly heart of Fr. Peter, love obedient and humble that has a very amazing power to attract others to God in order to bestow upon them the grace of salvation. *And when I am lifted up from the earth* [on the Cross], *I will draw everyone to myself*—says Lord Jesus.

Fr. Peter's obedience spoke volumes more than what he had done before.

Looking at how Fr. Peter currently serves people with his gift of intercessional prayer, I could touch and contemplate the love of Jesus crucified in the name of His obedience to God the Father—a strong love, being faithful until death; a victorious love leading to resurrrection. God's love found in Fr. Peter's heart manifests itself very much in a human way—with his attentive look, a friendly smile, a hug and, above all, by treating everyone personally, for the sake of that particular person. In the course of the intercessional prayer, Fr. Peter serves man, first of all, with the gift of Christ's love, which is patient, kind, not quick-tempered, not seeking its own interests, not brooding over injury, bearing all, and trusting all. By this love, he is in union with human hardship and suffering. By this love, he reveals the Crucified Jesus and beseeches His mercy for those who are unwell because they are laden with the suffering of body and soul.

I observed Fr. Peter during his many hours long ministry to people when he was sometimes extremely exhausted from physical strain, when he sensed the rail of the handrail behind him, leaning on it at least for a while, to give a little rest to his exhausted body. I saw him forced to sit down in the hallway to rest, while he was on the way to his room. For the last of the scheduled prayer meetings, he was already unable to come because the exertion proved to be extreme. In his ministry, so full of sacrifice for people, it was evident that, together with Christ, he was a good shepherd who gives his own life for the sheep in sacrifice for the salvation of another man. Despite his many hours' service and the extreme exhaustion, I did not notice any indication of impatience, complaint, or dissatisfaction in Fr. Peter's behavior. Just the opposite, his behavior was full of peace and kindness—his face expressed an authentic kindness, his eyes radiated with the brightness of his faith and love, his lips almost unceasingly hosted a wonderful smile, his moves and manner of behavior expressed the love of neighbor and brotherly closeness again and again.

People coming to the meeting with Fr. Peter were driven by the spirit of faith and trust in God—an atmosphere of praying and God's peace were predominant there. One could feel the close and special presence of Jesus. There was no panicky rough and tumble or sensational curiosity. There were many prayer vigils in quietude and silence; there was an expectation of Jesus Presence and His healing and curative grace. Through the faith of Fr. Peter and the congregated people, the presence of Jesus became more and more alive and close. Jesus healed, cured, filled up the hearts with the Grace of the Holy Spirit. Many persons experienced Resting in the Holy Spirit. All those who came, attracted to Fr. Peter by the love of Christ and a sincere desire for a transformation of their lives, were glad at the close presence of Jesus and the gift of unity in the Holy Spirit that they found they could experience at the prayer meeting.

Some people were afraid of meeting with Fr. Peter, however. Their lack of consent to a conversion and stubborn persistence in living in sin were the reasons why they did not wanted to come to the intercessional prayer. Many among those who were present at the church were speaking with bleeding hearts about their close relatives who had lost their friendship with Jesus and even abandoned the faith, and, for this reason, had not come to the prayer meeting. They were showing their photographs and asking for prayers for them.

Those who were the most afraid and panicked before meeting with Fr. Peter were demon-possessed people. For them, Fr. Peter appeared as a great threat. One person, Annie, was cursing Fr. Peter and threatening to kill him. Yet, after all, she was helped by the grace of the Merciful Jesus in coming to the meeting with Fr. Peter in hope that, thanks to his intercessional prayer, the Lord Jesus would perhaps set her free from demonic possession. On one hand, she feared Fr. Peter, feared his prayer and blessing, and wished to run away from the church; and, on the other hand, she desired the intercessional prayer by Fr. Peter so the saving power of Jesus would overcome the enslaving and imprisoning power of evil.

Having noticed this demon-possessed person, Father Peter stopped by her. Despite the late time and his great fatigue, he devoted a lot of time to Annie. He prayed over her long and fervently, blessed her with the Holy Sacrament and asked the Merciful Jesus for the grace of delivering her from the power of the devil. On Fr. Peter's face, I saw immense compassion for Annie who was so strongly oppressed by the demon. He bent over her with great love; he patiently accepted all the symptoms of aggression and hostility toward him. His heart was seized by sorrow over Annie whose freedom and use of consciousness was taken away by the demon—so he was there with her . . . unceasingly praying to Jesus who had overcome the ruler of this world with His own death on the Cross and Resurrection. Along with Fr. Peter, all the priests, seminarians, and the congregated laypersons also prayed. The prayer of faith and love was one of waging a fight with the brute force and aggression of the demon. The Anointment of the Sick was also administered. When the symptoms of the satanic force and aggression at last began to clearly weaken, Fr. Peter approached Annie, smiled at her very heartily and stretched his arms toward her in a gesture of invitation to encourage her to come closer to him, trusting that he would not do any harm to her, because he loved her and wished to help her. In the gesture of bending over the suffering Annie, with his extended arms and his smile, there was so much authentic love that she willingly and quickly got up, approached Fr. Peter and confidently hugged him. In Fr. Peter's fatherly hugging, she sensed that it was the Lord Himself who had stretched to her His paternal arms to bestow upon her His own love; that it was the Lord Jesus Himself who was clasping her to His Sacred

Heart. Although the hugging gesture was prolonged, Fr. Peter did not interrupt it, feeling how much Annie thirsted for the pure love of the Living God.

So it went in Lowicz.

Annie's second meeting with Fr. Peter, this time in Kraków, went on similarly—the manifestation of the possession and the patient prayers by Fr. Peter and all the people who were present at the church, as well as the blessing with the Holy Sacrament. So, again, the Merciful Lord Jesus began to reveal the saving power of His Love—the symptoms of the possession gradually weakened, replaced by calmness and quietude; her human consciousness came back together with peace and trust toward the people surrounding her as she came up with questions: "Is this Fr. Peter?" "Where is he?" And, when Fr. Peter drew nearer to her and extended his arms as a gesture of a heartfelt invitation: "Come! Do not be afraid! Lord Jesus calls you to Himself," Annie got up at once and clung to Fr. Peter with all her heart as a loving child would to its loving Father.

On the next day, with Fr. Stanislaw Kania's approval, Annie could once again meet shortly with Fr. Peter, exchange some words with him, and embrace him with all her heart.

In her own statements about the second meeting with Fr. Peter, Annie referred many times to the moment when he embraced her. Each time, she underlined emphatically that, until then, nobody in her whole life had shown her so much love in the gesture of the paternal hugging as Fr. Peter did. She could neither describe nor explain that, but it was visible more and more clearly that she had experienced human love as well as God's Love through the mediation of Fr. Peter. In the fatherly arms of Fr. Peter, she met with the Living God. Just then, she was awash with an abundant stream of mercy and grace that flowed onto her from depths of the Heart of God, and it was just then that the demon had to make room for the Holy Spirit and she felt delivered from the evil possession. The internal transformation which she had undergone by then was still uncovered, unknown to Fr. Peter. It was why he allowed her to come to a third prayer meeting scheduled for two days later. In his humility, he proposed that Annie perhaps should come along with her exorcist. Fr. Peter is not an exorcist but showed a great love for her. Lord Jesus used his priestly and paternal love for Annie to execute within her the act of delivering her from the possession as early as at the second meeting. The nearest two days bore fruit of numerous indications of the genuineness of that deliverance. In that way, the Lord Jesus showed that the greatest power of the delivery of man from a devilish possession is found in the sincere and profound love shown to him.

Annie's third coming to see Fr. Peter was already in the spirit of thanksgiving for the grace of her deliverance. Before her second trip to the meeting with Fr. Peter, Annie had experienced many instances of internal resistance to going there, many fears of the meeting, and great resentment of Fr. Peter. When the meeting actually took place, all of those negative feelings simply vanished. Peace and joy dominated her thinking about the third meeting as she spoke about it with great love. She was waiting patiently for the meeting, while praying together with the entire congregation of the faithful at the church.

By then, Fr. Peter was for several hours serving unceasingly with his intercessional prayer, because there were so many persons asking for it. He was extremely exhausted, to the limit of his physical strength. Toward the end, he stopped a little longer, however, by Annie to give her a blessing. When she was resting in the Holy Spirit, he stood by, waiting patiently until Annie regained her full consciousness and, then, hugged her despite his total exhaustion. Concerned about his health, the persons accompanying him tried to shorten the gesture gently, but Fr. Peter would not concede, sensing that this child of God was very much in thirst of his priestly and fatherly love. Later on, at the church, Annie delivered her public testimony about the grace of her deliverance from possession.

Thanks be to God!

Fr. J., a Catholic Seminary Professor

Veni Sancte Spiritus

I am going in the direction of the church to check out if everything is buttoned up. After all, I am scheduled to perform my turn of duty in the Sacristy today. It is only 2 PM, and at 6 PM there will be a Eucharistic meeting held with Fr. Peter, an American charismatic priest, through whom God works miracles on both the body and the soul. I see a small group of people standing in front of the closed door; actually, they are standing and sitting, as some of them have arrived here in wheelchairs. So I open up the upper church earlier than I have planned and return to the Sacristy. I spend about 20 minutes there, and then I go out again to the Presbytery and—I can't believe my eyes—all the sitting spots in the pews are taken, except for several reserved seats up front. I return excited and continue to prepare for the Holy Mass.

The "Chaplet to the Divine Mercy" starts, followed by the exposition of the Holy Sacrament and Holy Confession for those who need it. One and a half hours have already passed, and I see the need for opening up the lower church, because the upper one is already filled up. Another hour passes, and I must go back to the Home of the Novitiate for a moment. I enter the home, and whom do I see? Father Peter and his entourage. I go forward to welcome him. Then he asks me who I am around here and wishes all good to me. I feel that this moment is very important to me. I see the simplicity, humility, and naturalness emanating from Father. After a while, I return to my own duties, however.

The paralyzed woman on a stretcher, who was supposed to be brought from the hospital is already here. The empty space in the Sacristy is becoming more and more scarce; it is getting crowded here. The remaining 20 minutes prior to the Holy Mass, are especially apprehensive. At last we make the opening sign of the cross. Then it is time for the homily. Father Peter approaches the pulpit and shouts: ALLELUIAH!!! This word resounds again—three times. There is no need to translate the word; we all know what it means. Father underlined in his sermon that it is God who does the healing of the sick, that we pursue toward Him, and that the most important healing is that of the spirit, not that of the body, because we all must die, anyway. The Eucharistic Liturgy begins.

At this time, Urszula, yet unknown to me, as she has arrived along with Fr. Peter, calls all the firemen and Piarist novices to the Sacristy and begins to explain to them about Resting in the Holy Spirit. I do not get the whole idea, but I wait patiently for what will occur. It is the end of the Eucharist. Now the healing service begins, during which Fr. Peter blesses the faithful. Earlier on, however, all of them repeat the words of the healing prayer with their eyes set on the Cross. Then Fr. Peter anoints the faithful. Many of them fall on the floor in a semi-sleep state; those who are falling down are helped by the novices and firemen. They lay for some time, then get up and leave.

Unexpectedly, something new happens to us—the manifestations of two demonic possessions in two youths, a boy and a girl. Satan makes his presence felt. After a while, I see both youths lying on the carpets in the Presbytery. One of the Fathers exposes the Holy Sacrament. At this moment, the attacks of the demon intensify. Lightly frightened, we pray with faith anyway.

After a couple of hours, when everyone has already received the blessing, Fr. Stanisław Kania (a Piarist, one of the co-organizers of Fr. Peter's tour in Poland), asks the members of a Spiritual Renewal Group to remain and pray for the deliverance of these two youths. Fr. Janusz, who presides over the prayer, begins to sing *Veni Sancte Spiritus*. It is visible now how much Satan dislikes these words. Finally, everything calms down. The youths join the faithful in prayer. However, a long fight still awaits them, as the evil spirits have not left them yet.

It is already quite past midnight. Going to bed, I thank God for so great a grace that He has bestowed upon so many people today. I entrust everything to God, and I know already that this has been one of the most important days in my life.

Jesus gave his disciples an authority over the demons and the power to forgive sins. Father Peter is, with no doubt, a man through whom God acts in a tangible way.

What I witnessed during this event strengthened my faith but also gave me much to think about. It is important, however, not to keep those experiences for myself but to share them, especially with those who are skeptical about the phenomenon of evil possession.

It has not come as a surprise to me that Satan is active, but never did I experience so tangibly the signs of his activity, and I've become assured that he is unusually hideous.

We all need the Divine Mercy, prayer, and continuous healing by the Power of God. At the end of this testimony, I encourage everyone to say with faith *The Miracle Prayer*, written by Fr. Peter, every day, irrespective of how we feel.

Andrzej Skrzek, a seminarian

It Was an Important Moment on the Way of My Novitiate Formation

I have been a novice at the Order of the Piarist Fathers in Rzeszów since September 11, 2004. In December of that year, a landmark event happened for the entire local community of the Novitiate and the parish—the visit of Fr. Peter Mary Rookey. What I experienced then will stay in my memory for a very long time. Despite my deep faith in God, I never imagined how strongly God can act through other people. Until that day, I was very skeptical about such things like the healing of people's bodies and souls. The December events firmly opened my eyes to that issue.

On that day, the church was crowded with people. Everybody came in with their own problems. At about 6 PM, the Holy Mass started. Father Peter blessed everyone with his own crucifix and anointed each individual with the Holy Oil. The faithful experienced miracles. As in so many other places, the crippled began to walk. The first persons who were blessed were the priests and the liturgical attendants. I gradually started to realize that the meeting with Fr. Peter was a tremendous experience for me. I am aware of the fact that so much good came my way at such a crucial moment on my path of my novitiate formation. What I experienced during the meeting with Fr. Peter gave me living evidence that Jesus really loves us.

Darek, a novice

I Considered Demonic Possession a Funny Thing

I have been a novice in the Order of the Piarists Schools in Rzeszów since September 11, 2004. I found out about the meeting with Fr. Peter from the parish announcements at our church. It was made known that an American charismatic priest, Fr. Peter Mary Rookey, OSM, was coming to us and that a Holy Mass would be celebrated for the healing of the body and soul for all people. I did not believe in any miraculous healing and considered demonic possession a funny thing. Day by day, Fr. Peter's arrival was drawing nearer; day by day, there were more preparations and more people calling us up with questions. Finally, the day arrived. People began to gather as early as 1 PM, although the beginning of the whole event was planned to start at 5 PM. At about 4 PM, the upper church was full and people went down to the lower church. During the Holy Mass, Fr. Peter preached in English, of course, and his sermon was translated to Polish. After the Holy Mass, the service began during which Fr. Peter blessed and anointed everybody.

The first persons whom Fr. Peter blessed did not experience anything, and I began to think that every bit of what was said about Resting in the Holy Spirit was nothing but some invention. But it started to happen. When the first person fell down on me, I did not know what was going on. Suddenly I heard a scream of some boy and it turned out to be a case of demonic possession. Here, really deep prayers for his healing were started. Soon there was another person, a girl this time. They were both carried to the Presbytery. Some of the Fathers asked for the Monstrance, and the Holy Sacrament was exposed, in front of which a special prayer started. One could say that we were holding not a man but a devil who jumped, wriggled, and yelled. It intensified especially after bringing those two individuals near the Holy Sacrament and sprinkling them with Holy Water. At that time, I did not think of what was happening; I did what I was told to do. When all that ended, the congregation and the young people from this parish still continued to pray.

I did not start to reflect on everything until the second day. And I went on throughout the evening and the next day not quite aware of what was really going on with me. That meeting strengthened my faith and made me sure that Satan could bring man to a horrible state. It depends only on our choice which shape of life awaits us—with the Merciful God, or with Satan—the ruler of darkness.

Oleg, a novice

The Desire for the Meeting and . . . Fear of It

I have been a novice in the Order of the Piarist Fathers since September 2004. The Home of the Novitiate is located in the Parish of the Piarist Fathers in Rzeszów. Thanks to that, since the moment of our arrival at the novitiate, we, the novices, have had an opportunity not only to witness the life of the parish from the inside, but also to actively participate in its life.

Herein, I would like to share my impressions and very deep experiences related to the visit of a charismatic priest, Fr. Peter Mary, to our parish. One Sunday in November, during the pastoral announcements, our parish priest, Fr. Wojciech, announced an arrival of a monk from America at our parish. "Father Peter Rookey (the parish priest read out loud) will come to our parish on December 15, 2004." We, the novices, did not know much about him really; just that he was of partially Irish origin, was a charismatic, and healed people. We would surely be satisfied for a long time with only such information except for the fact that more and more people were calling up the novitiate for specific information. At the beginning, we could say little to them. Over time, however, we managed to obtain a little more information on Fr. Peter's ministry and life.

I must say that I was awed when I found out about the numerous healings taking place through the ministry of that priest. On the one hand, I wanted very much to experience meeting this man; on the other hand, however, I was afraid. The endless telephone calls were a sign of very great interest in the person of this priest and the upcoming meeting.

To accommodate the church space for admitting as great a number of people as possible, it was necessary to arrange additional benches. We also had to reserve spaces for persons in wheelchairs as it was self-evident that such persons would also want to attend the meeting.

For the faithful who wanted to participate in the Holy Mass concelebrated by Fr. Peter, the door of the church was to be open at about 3:00 PM. However, the first people appeared in front of the church as early as 1:30 PM. The church filled up double-quick. Still long before 6:00 PM, the scheduled hour of the commencement of the Eucharist, the church was full, yet the people continued to arrive.

At about 5:00 PM, the Rosary prayer started, and all the novices were waiting in the Sacristy for Fr. Peter's arrival. Several minutes later, one of the persons who, as we later found out accompanied Fr. Peter during his preceding meetings at other parishes, came to the Sacristy. In a short conversation with us, she told us about extraordinary phenomena that accompany Father's blessing. She spoke about Resting in the Holy Spirit, loud crying, and people shouting while accepting the blessing. Whereas I could somehow explain rationally to myself the crying or screaming, Resting in the Holy Spirit was something unusual and inexplicable to me. Yet, pretty soon, I was to become a witness to those inconceivable phenomena.

And it came to pass. After the end of the Eucharist, during which Fr. Peter said a homily, we were asked to help with carrying people on wheelchairs to the Presbytery. For a long time, I will remember the faces of those people. Especially the face of one woman who, encouraged and supported by Fr. Peter after receiving the blessing, got up from her wheelchair and, held up by him, made several steps. In that moment, tears appeared not only on the face of this woman but could also be seen in the eyes of other people.

However, the most shocking to me, and which I will certainly keep in my memory forever, was the view of a boy looking about 17, lying on the church floor, who reacted with a loud scream several minutes after having received a blessing. It was evident that he was losing his control over his own body, because he was assuming very strange positions. His behavior drew the attention of all the people gathered in the church. When Fr. Rookey stood up close by him and began to recite the deliverance prayers, I realized that the boy was possessed by an evil spirit. I and my fellow brothers, all tried to stop the youngster's wriggling on the church floor. It was hard to predict his next reactions, especially to the Holy Sacrament, with which Fr. Peter started to bless him. A moment later, the youngster's girlfriend started to show signs of demonic possession. Fr. Peter recited the deliverance prayers over her, too.

All this lasted for several hours. One could see expressions of horror on the faces of many people gathered in the church. Despite his visible fatigue, Fr. Peter continued the prayers, accompanied by the loud prayer of the congregation.

Never before had I seen anything like it. I was overtaken by great fear and nervousness but, at some moments, when I was looking at Fr. Peter, I experienced some internal calm and security emanating from his peaceful face and his securing presence among us.

When I had an opportunity to talk with those youths shortly before midnight, it seemed to me, for a moment, that I had been dreaming. Only a dozen or so minutes earlier, I—together with my fellow brothers—had been holding the boy reeling on the carpet, and now he was standing close by me. As if nothing had ever happened, he was telling me about his own experiences. When I was leaving the church, I did not quite know what to think about what I had seen. When at home, after having had a supper with Fr. Peter, I could not fall asleep for long hours. I still saw the figures of those youths before my eyes. Scenes from this meeting were passing in my memory like a movie. I felt an urgent need to go to our household chapel. I wanted to put it all in some order within myself; I wanted to stay alone with the Lord Jesus.

So many times did I read in the Gospel the fragments about demon-possessed persons delivered by Jesus. That evening, Fr. Peter's ministry gave me an opportunity to be an eyewitness to a real case of what I had only read about. I am grateful to the Lord that I could participate in this unusual meeting with Fr. Peter and experience the Presence of Jesus Himself through Father's ministry just at the beginning of my path toward the monastic life.

Godspeed!

Piotr, a novice

I Asked for the Healing of My Faith

I found out about Father Peter and his arrival at our parish community from Father Rector's pastoral announcements in mid-November 2004. At the beginning, I was not interested in it in a special way. I thought that a senior preacher would come, one of many. After what happened then, I must confess that I was very wrong. Initially, I did not take seriously all the things that we were told. However, the less time that remained until Father's arrival, more news reaching our community began to fill me with interest in him. I went about more and more excited and began to believe in this more and more. I asked God to deepen my faith within me and make my spiritual vocation greater through Fr. Peter's blessing. Several days prior to his arrival, I learned about the healings, Resting in the Holy Spirit, and demonic possessions that were witnessed to in a couple of other places that Fr. Peter had already visited before he came to Rzeszów.

On the day of his arrival, as the hour of his arrival at our parish was drawing nearer and nearer, I was getting more and more anxious and curious as to what would occur in our local parish. Finally, the waiting was over. The monk got out of the car, and it was apparent that he was tired. When he entered the Home of the Novitiate, he looked at me and greeted me warmheartedly. Right off, it was evident that he was not just a monk but a great man. Before the beginning of the Holy Mass celebrated by Fr. Stanislaw, thanks to whom we had the honor to meet Fr. Peter, Urszula informed us about what could occur during the blessing; namely, about Resting in the Holy Spirit, people crying or weeping, and about demonic possessions.

The Holy Mass began with a half-hour delay. Fr. Peter delivered a sermon. After the Holy Mass, the ministry, for which everyone had been waiting, started. Fr. Peter blessed the priests first, then the sick waiting in the Sacristy. After coming back to the Presbytery, he blessed us (the novices), the liturgical assistants, and firemen who were helping the people in wheelchairs during the blessing and keeping an order during the blessings of the faithful. My and my fellow brothers' task was catching and putting down the people who were falling down to rest in the Holy Spirit. Everything was happening as it had been foretold to us before the service. I was totally shocked when I saw the first people resting in the Holy Spirit. After some time, I heard screaming and was called out by one of our Fathers to prepare the Monstrance to expose the Holy Sacrament, because there were two demon-possessed persons. Since then, when I saw what was happening, time came to a standstill for me. I joined my fellow brothers who were holding up the possessed people and praying over them for their deliverance. In the latter part of the whole event, the people who stayed in the church started to pray for the possessed people as well. I became certain with my very own eyes what faith and the communal prayer are all about. I knew for sure since that moment nobody is going to tell me that there is no Satan and no evil—he is there and stays vigilant *like a roaring lion, seeking whom to devour.*

After coming home, we sat down to a common supper and we re-lived what had occurred at the church. After the supper, we were blessed once again by Fr. Peter. Somewhere around 4 AM I awoke and only then did it begin to get to me what had occurred and in what God had permitted me, an ordinary 20-something-year-old novice still at the start of his formation, to participate. I felt fear and anxiety, knowing not against what or whom. What I felt inside myself is indescribable. In the morning, I was not able to function well. I could not help but think only about what had happened in the preceding day's evening. It was explained to me that I had nothing to fear since, after all, I receive Holy Communion every day and I am protected by God and my Guardian Angel.

Before, it had always appeared to me like, "what a big deal, some devil." I had read a little on the subject but, even in my most daring imagination, I did not suppose it could be such a power. Now, after a month since those events, I have been asked to write about what I had experienced then, and my heart is jumping like crazy. I only know this much—I asked for the healing of my faith and I surely received it. From that time on, I have had a completely different approach to life and some issues. I thank God that He put me in that place at that time. I am grateful to one more person who helped me, although partly, come back to my senses after those events. Before noon, shortly ahead of the extraordinary Father's leaving, we were blessed once again. Since then, I ask God and I pray to him for more such persons as Fr. Peter Rookey and the persons who accompanied him.

Godspeed!

Przemek, a novice

The Witness of an Altar Boy
(a Hand-written Letter)

Rzeszów, February 12, 2005

On the day when Fr. Peter visited our parish (December 15, 2004), I went to the church to serve at the Holy Mass. I liked very much the words that Fr. Peter turned to us in the sermon. After the Holy Mass, Fr. Peter was blessing the sick and he touched me on that occasion. Subsequently, I felt like I was electrocuted and, then, fainted. I had to sit down. Ever since then, I have been speaking better and better and my stuttering has decreased.

I thank God for what I have gone through by saying 10 Hail Marys of the Rosary and taking part in Holy Masses everyday. I also would like to ask for further graces by saying Fr. Peter's prayer.

Mateusz Oczos
Age, 11 years

We, the parents, do certify that everything that our son has written herein is true. We also adore God for His grace.

The parents: Marta Oczos
Jacek Oczos

THE PEACE THAT GOD GIVES US UNSPARINGLY

Father Peter Mary Rookey was scheduled to visit our parish on Wednesday, December 15, 2005. To tell the truth, we went to the meeting completely unprepared. We neither had much information about him, nor imagined quite accurately the kind of service that we were going to experience. In addition, we were experiencing some serious concerns then and our participation in Mass solemnities of that kind was the last thing that we wished for. We only knew that we would be attending a more solemn Holy Mass celebrated for the intention of healing the sick. Today, we think that our ignorance had its own purpose. As a matter of fact, we were able to begin the evening without expecting any unusual and extraordinary events and, as a result, we were able to participate in something far beyond a routine very important occurrence, which was proved to be.

When the time of the meeting was coming close, our not too big church was, so to speak, "bursting at the seams." It was getting filled by crowds of people, including those carted in wheelchairs and those with visible sufferings of body and soul.

Father Peter turned out to be a medium-size, gray-haired elderly, yet lively, man exuding love, peace and—above all—vast, almost contagious, joy. Most of the people present there were moved by the enthusiasm with which he was speaking about God and His love. In the homily, he reminded everyone about the truth that we often forget—that the Lord has a great power with which He heals the sick, delivers us from evil, and washes away our sins and weaknesses every day. Father Rookey also reminded us that the foundation of all healing is forgiveness, which is mentioned in *The Miracle Prayer* arranged by him:

> . . . *I am sorry for my sins, I repent of my sins, please forgive me.*
> *In Your Name I forgive all others for what they have done against me* . . . .

The Holy Mass was followed by a service, in which Father Peter intended to give individual blessings to all the faithful. With slight disbelief, we listened to the remarks of the organizers informing us of what might occur; about many people who would rest in the Holy Spirit, and about the sick who might become healed. And so it happened. Before our very eyes, the power of the Living Christ was revealed, giving His amazing graces through the means of this inconspicuous man of big heart. We saw the sick getting up from their wheelchairs, we perceived many persons experiencing their special meetings with God through Resting in the Holy Spirit, we prayed for two youths to be freed by the Lord from demonic possession. We ourselves experienced special feelings of unity in prayer, reconciliation, and forgiveness for those who had wronged us one way or another. The blessing given to us by Fr. Peter poured into our hearts the peace taken away from us by other people, peace that God gives us unsparingly if only we ask and wait for it confidently. In some sense, that day contributed to the strengthening of our faith and made us aware of the power of Christ. Fr. Peter was inscribed in our hearts as an example of a Man of Faith and a True Disciple of Jesus. Today we return to the Gospel that was read on that day and we admire the phenomenon of the incessant validity of the Word in which God directed us just then and confirmed in the person of Fr. Peter, *And he said to them in reply, "Go and tell John what you have seen and heard: the blind regain their sight, the lame walk, lepers are cleansed, the deaf hear, the dead are raised, the poor have the good news proclaimed to them. And blessed is the one who takes no offense at me* (Lk 7:22-23).

Gabriela and Piotr

Resting in the Holy Spirit and Demonic Possession

As usual, I do not know where to start, so I will introduce myself. I do not come from this parish, not even from Rzeszów, but my own curiosity and the warmth directly radiating from this parish have made me take part in the life of this church for over 1 year. That Fr. Peter Rookey would be a guest at the Piarists at the Wilkowyja district of Rzeszow on Wednesday, December 15, 2004, I had known about a month earlier, but, in the multitude of current matters and everyday problems, I completely forgot about it. In that way, the month had passed fast, almost like a week.

On a Wednesday morning, I was busy at college and I planned on going to a Holy Mass at 6:00 PM. I knew that it would be concelebrated by Fr. Rookey (a charismatic priest), and that, after the Holy Mass, there would be a ceremony of the anointing of the faithful, during which one could experience a moment of personal meeting with God (the so-called Resting in the Holy Spirit) and, as I had expected, everything was to go in an ordinary way.

Right from the start, however, my hopes became dissipated by Fr. Wojciech's request that I play some canons from Taizé during Fr. Peter's anointing of the faithful. There was no time to gather people who, by the way, appeared later (probably by a decree of Providence). When I came to the Mass, both the upper and the lower churches were filled to the brim. I somehow arranged to procure a guitar (courtesy of seminarian Andrew). Thanks to the guitar giving me some "importance," I succeeded in entering the church through the Sacristy and took a position on the right side of the altar stairs. I had no time to prepare the repertoire, either, since the Holy Mass was just starting. I have to admit that I was browsing the songbooks while listening to the sermons to choose the compositions appropriate to the content preached by Fr. Peter. I was very uneasy with the approaching end of the Holy Mass and the fact that there still was no one else but me to play guitar and sing. My heart was relieved when Mr. Wasacz said that he would try to find my wife who was somewhere in the church. Magnificent!—It would make at least two.

It started! Already during the "Chaplet to the Divine Mercy," we were, unexpectedly, anointed by Fr. Peter. It happened so suddenly that it did not occur to me that had we been able to experience Resting in the Holy Spirit, who would have been there to do the singing? Despite the lack of any initial plan of the musical compositions, our singing went quite well. The center of the church and sideways to the altar steps, along which the anointed people moved, were behind me when I played. During intervals, when the chaplet was said, I saw firemen and novices who were helping people in wheelchairs and catching those who were falling down on the church floor to protect them from hurting their bodies.

I slowly lost the sense of time, but it seems to me that, after an hour or so, I heard something like crying and I thought it was a sick child or a senior citizen experiencing a healing and getting emotionally moved. Only when Fr. Kania ordered us to stop playing, did I understand what had occurred. I had read books about this topic, I had seen movies, but those were words and images only, while, here, I had a chance to observe "live" what it meant when demons try to be the master of a human soul. There were two young persons, maybe 17-year-olds, lying in the Presbytery, and Fr. Peter and the other priests were praying over them for their deliverance.

Because I do not feel quite competent to further impart what I saw and experienced, I will only say this much. The event shook me so much that I had to seriously reflect over the condition of my faith. It was good that I did not have to sleep that night alone in an empty, dark house; here I thank those who saved me from that, because I probably would have gone out of my senses. I will remember what I lived through for my entire life as an admonition. I thank God for giving me the opportunity of having such an experience, and for the internal peace that He bestows upon me whenever I need it; for making it happen, standing in the close imminence of the Christmas holidays, when we need so much a testimony that Christ is always present in the community and comes to our aid whenever we need it; for the fact that experiencing such an event strengthens the ties between its participants and tempers the spirit, I could see with own eyes the power of the Body of Our Savior concealed in a "piece of bread" and realize what can be achieved by the mediation of Mary and the Saints; and for the fact that God makes me realize all the time that I am but "a grain of dust and a leaf in the wind" and thereby He tames my pride.

Krzysztof Martyniuk

I Found the Courage to Go to Confession

I came to Father Peter's prayer meeting not out of curiosity, but rather, as a person stricken by many long-term diseases. I did not count on receiving any blessing. I had stayed out of confession for 2 years. It was the Advent time then, and the beginning of the Christmas season.

As soon as I heard *The Miracle Prayer* said before the Holy Cross, I felt that something was happening to me. My eyes were fixed upon the Cross, my heart was palpitating, and my hands started to tremble. While walking up to receive the blessing, I knew—I just do not know how—that I was going to fall. I wanted to look into Father's eyes when he would be coming up to me, but I do not remember that very moment at all. I was conscious when lying down; my eyelids were blinking quickly, my heart was pounding. And, I felt very, very comfortable; so much so that I wanted the sensation to last indefinitely.

Once I got back home, I first looked for the Cross on the walls; I had forgotten by then where it was hanging and, yet, I desired so much to see it. I behaved in the same way for the next couple of days, although I felt about it day by day less intensively. Yet, I felt as if my heart were awakened to a great love and yearning out of my whole life of dreaming; then, it was little by little put back to sleep again.

I did not have the prayer that Father recommended to say. I got a copy of it a few days later, but, anyhow, with my life so filled with haste and daily responsibilities, I lacked the consistency to actually say it. My diseases did not fade away, but I did not expect that at all. I found the courage to go to confession, and I think this is the most important thing that happened. It is only sad that I cannot evoke that wonderful feeling and sense of a beautiful longing within me again.

Aldona

I Experienced Two Miracles: One Greater and One Lesser

My name is Fr. Stefan Denkiewicz. I belong to the educational order that bears the name of the Order of the Pious Schools, in short—the Piarists. I teach foreign languages at our novitiate in Rzeszów; I help at the Parish of St. Joseph Calasantius in this city; sometimes I translate texts from foreign languages to Polish; I write and publish novels for children and youngsters. It is quite a bit for the 72-year-old priest that I am.

But this is not what worried me then. In general, I am a cheerful man, sometimes even very much so, which is reflected in my meetings with young people and in the adventures described in my novels. Unfortunately, the cheerfulness of my life and the joy that I derive from small things have been overshadowed more and more in the last years by a certain disease. Something like a magnet was pulling me leftward, sometimes making me stagger in both the left and the right directions. Many times it was so strong that I had to return home after passing 100 yards on my way, so as not to astonish anyone or raise suspicions among the passers-by. It was a disease of the labyrinth.

After several years, the disease went into its next phase. It attacked me suddenly causing impulsive, short-lived wobbling from which I had to seek recourse by way of making a very quick jump and stamping with my legs. This was unpleasant to do while lecturing in the novitiate, and openly dangerous—especially when distributing Holy Communion to the faithful at church. Many times, I had to lean on people and wait until it passed. Sometimes, the congregation was thinking that I was lame. I offered up this Cross of mine to God, and I tried to be careful to take into my hands those chalices in which there were only a few hosts to reduce the possibility of dropping them.

Fr. Peter Mary Rookey came to us in Rzeszów. It was on a cold evening on December 15, 2004. There were crowds of people in the choir balcony. The upper and the lower church was filled up with people as well, even though we did not put out printed flyers throughout the city, suspecting that too many people would come in and we would not be able to manage the situation.

I confess people, but only a few persons could get through the crowd to reach the confessional. So I am praying in this spare time, I am praying, but . . . not for health. I am praying for a transformation of my spirituality at a certain point; to put it more specifically, for a faithfulness to a certain small part of my prayer and its invigoration by the spirit of love. I pray so, I pray seriously and, afterwards, I listen to Fr. Peter's cheerful homily. How many times it is interspersed with joyful Alleluiahs! How joyful are the healings of bodies that God does for the people; but even more important are the transformations of spirit and the faithfulness to Christ. How strongly Fr. Peter puts it in our hearts that there is no Christianity or even human nature without forgiveness and concern for love . . .

I approached Fr. Peter after the Holy Mass, not at the beginning of the blessings but some time later. I knelt down before him and asked in Italian for a blessing. Hearing the sound of my request in Italian, he smiled at me (I felt that hearing that language pleased him), touched my head on both sides and blessed me; I got up satisfied and left.

I prayed a lot both solely and with other people, especially for two demon-possessed youngsters but, at 10 PM, I went to sleep to be able to work the next day; Father followed considerably later, since he was greatly beleaguered by the people and prayed with them for so long.

On the second day, I spoke with him in Italian at the table. He was appreciative of the faith of the Polish people, talked about his Irish origin, and about faith. He remembered the time he spent in Rome when he was young, listened, and we exchanged views on many topics. With other people, he spoke in English.

What will I say in the end? After all, I began to write to bear witness. Here it is:

I experienced two miracles. One was bigger, the other one was lesser. The greater, more important one, was the joy from being faithful to that tiny part of prayer that was troublesome to me; from being faithful, indeed, from the moment of receiving the blessing to this day. I know that I am faithful to this tiny part; I feel that it is dear to me, and I am convinced that this is not owing to myself but it has come to me as a gift from the Best Father through the hands of His child Peter.

The second miracle is lesser but sufficient for me. Something happened in my body. On the next day after receiving the blessing, I did not even once have to jump up to keep up my balance. Walking inside the house, in the yard, and at the church, I was not swaying from side to side, I felt normal and confident. Only when I was going out for a longer walk, did I feel something minor happening inside me. While walking down a sidewalk in the city, I had an impression that it was slightly shaking under my feet as if it were afloat, but I have to stress that the vacillation was very gentle. That phenomenon lasted for a month or so.

Now, I do not observe it in me anymore. It will appear at times all of a sudden, however, but only as some very light tremor that I overcome instinctively by stomping my feet. However—as I emphasize—it is very weak and unnoticeable by people. It does not appear often, either; sometimes it will not appear at all for a week or a little longer, unlike in the past, when it used to seize me many times daily, and in an acute way.

The Mercy of the Lord I shall sing forever!

Written on February 22, 2005

Fr. Stefan Denkiewicz, SchP,*
125 Lwowska Street, 35-301 Rzeszów, Poland

Postscriptum [*added on March 26, 2005, Holy Saturday*]
I share my joy after further improvement of my health. I bless the Lord that, in His Kindness, He has been extending until today, and continues to do so, what He began in mid-December 2004 through His servant Peter. I really feel better and better. I serve the faithful while moving about the church, more and more firm in my steps. I do not lose my balance when I am in my apartment or delivering lectures, which can be confirmed by the novices. I do not go out much to the city, because I am very busy, but I feel better making the small walks. Thanks be to God for everything! I also give thanks to all the people, thanks to whom I met His so privileged servant, Fr. Peter Mary.

---

*   I agree, and even ask the Publishers, to include my address under my testimony.

I Was Not Praying for Myself

On the day of December 15, 2004, I attended a service at the church of the Piarists in Rzeszów. I had never before prayed incessantly for so long (from 5:00 PM to 10:00 PM). By now, I know that it was an immense grace—the grace of being totally absorbed in prayer.

For the first time ever, I was also a witness to prayers for deliverance from demonic possessions and to an enormous transformation in a young boy after a demon was cast out of him. At first, he howled and roared; he was flinging himself and rolling over the church floor. It went on similarly with the second person—a young girl, his girlfriend. It lasted for about 2 to 3 hours. And, at last, after prolonged prayers, there came that great transformation. I still see the smile of the young man, his bright face, and the thankfulness with which he simply "threw himself" into Fr. Peter's arms to express his gratitude by this gesture.

I also experienced the grace of Resting in the Holy Spirit during the individual blessing by Fr. Peter. Somebody lifted me up after some time and placed me in a pew, while I continued to feel the great bliss and wished this feeling would never end.

From that time on, the rebirth of my soul began to have an effect. I smile and rejoice more often. My family and the people close to me have already noticed this. The Rosary prayer is a joy to me! I wish to thank everyone who has helped me in my life and ask for forgiveness from those whom I have hurt.

I would like to mention that I had suffered from a deep depression earlier on and underwent some medical treatment; I had by then been taking strong psychotropic drugs for 3 months. The problems that had led me to depression now appear to me as something insignificant. Nay! Almost joyful! Isn't it strange?

Thanks be to You, Jesus! Thanks be to You, Mary, who have led me to this great transformation because I had earlier visited You at Medjugorje (in summer)! Thank you, Fr. Peter, for having come to Rzeszow; it was a privilege to be there all the way through your service. It is a great and visible grace—this strengthening of my faith, for which I have always asked, and now have turned into my total trust in Jesus and Mary.

I prayed all along during the service, for the intention of my niece Dorota, mother of three little children, who had a cancer. I commended her to the Divine Mercy. After the Holy Mass, I prayed with all the faithful for the delivery of that young boy from the devil. And . . . the one who experienced the healing was I myself!

It is impossible to express or describe with words those great spiritual experiences, those transformations. After all, they were felt very strongly and they stay with me; but to convey them into the soul of another person is not easy.

Also, I will not forget Fr. Peter lying prostrate in front of the altar. This lasted so long that I had thought that it would never end. Then, he bent over those poor demon-possessed people lying on the floor—a boy and a girl—holding a Monstrance with the Most Holy Sacrament in his hands and calling "Jesus!", "Mary!"; he almost touched this boy with the Monstrance, and the boy—held up by several men—was roaring all the time with a voice not sounding like a human voice. Sometimes I close my eyes and I see that still in the same way and as clearly as if it were happening today. My heart was seized by an anxiety: what if the demon will not get out of him? I wanted to cry and I prayed even more fervently, of course, under the leadership of the priest and the whole church.

That's that in brief.

The joy of life has filled me. I was in such despair previously and feared that I might have ended up in a mental institution. I asked God to keep me away from it.

I feel that I am a new person, completely changed. Yet, I know that, at that time, when I was not praying for myself, I utterly forgot about my depression and other ailments. I was asking for my young niece and for that poor, shrieking boy. I was very sorry for him.

Once again, I thank you wholeheartedly, Fr. Peter, for your words, for your smile, for your being there. I wish with all my changed heart and soul that Good God will keep you in good health and bless your works.

With immense gratitude and assurance of remembering you, dear Father, in my prayers,

Jaroslawa,
a school teacher

The above testimony was accompanied by two medical certificates.

I Went There Rather Out of Curiosity

I am 63 years old. Like many persons of my age, I suffer from various diseases. For a dozen or so years, I have been undergoing a treatment for arterial hypertension, have developed some degenerative arthritic changes in my joints and otosclerosis in my left ear, and have been taking antiasthmatic drugs. For more than a half year, I had had an upset stomach, frequent diarrheas, and steadily intensifying nausea after eating. I tried to heal myself using household remedies, because I feared very much to mention those ailments to the doctor.

It was announced in our parish that, on December 15, 2004, a Holy Mass would be celebrated with the participation of a charismatic priest, Fr. Peter Mary Rookey. My close family and friends did not mention much to me about the ministry or the miraculous healings happening through the prayers of this expected, dignified guest, Fr. Rookey. My internal voice, however, was saying that I should go to the meeting. So, as the only person from my family (I have a husband, two sons, daughters-in-law, and two grandsons), I resolved to go to the Rosary and the Holy Mass followed by the ministry of Fr. Peter. It could be said that I went there out of curiosity, rather than with an expectation of receiving the grace of healing.

I entered the church at 4:00 PM; it was very crowded by then. All the seats were taken, and the crowd of standing people was packed like sardines in a can. I pushed forward through the crowd toward the front section of the church and stood there until 9:00 PM. Nevertheless, despite standing there all along, I felt very strong and well. During the Holy Mass for the intention of healing, I prayed especially for the grace of having even deeper faith for myself and the other members of my family. I took part in that splendid service with keen devotion and immense concentration; I desired every word expressed by the servant of God, Fr. Peter, to fall deeply into my heart so it could change. At about 9:00 PM, I was blessed by Fr. Peter with a special crucifix containing the relics of saints. And, right there, I experienced something unexpected, something inconceivable to me. Immediately after the blessing, I felt in my belly a very strong pain that went on when I was walking through the church and then around the church. I understood that it was an extraordinary sign of the charismatic ministry of the servant of Christ, Fr. Peter Mary.

Ever since that memorable evening, I have had no nausea, I can eat everything. I have also noticed that my strong fits of coughing have faded away and I have put away my drugs for asthma. Now I know for sure that it was the Lord and His Sacred Mother who brought me to the Service of that dignified servant of Christ so that I would be able to experience so evidently the nearness, presence, and the Infinite Love of the Most High God. Since that meeting, I have been saying the prayer for healing every day. I often pray for the health and the necessary graces for Fr. Peter. Through all my life, the Lord and His Sacred Mother have been bestowing upon unworthy me, countless graces, leading me along His own paths. However, what I experienced that evening has surpassed my expectations.

I know no words with which I can thank the Lord God for the sign received through the ministry of Fr. Peter, a great and dignified Servite.

Unworthy Joanna

A Christmas Gift From Heaven

In December 2004, I began to celebrate Our Lord's coming down to Earth earlier than I did in the past. That year it started on Wednesday evening, December 15. On that day, I received the most beautiful holiday gift of my life, a genuine little star from Heaven. I attended a Holy Mass concelebrated by Fr. Peter Mary Rookey in my parish church, St. Joseph Calasantius Church in Rzeszów. The church had been crowded since the early hours. The faithful were praying the Rosary and the Chaplet to the Divine Mercy, and they were singing songs.

In his homily, Fr. Peter talked about the numerous miraculous healings that Jesus had worked through his mediation. Father Peter emphasized that the prerequisite condition for a healing to occur was to forgive everyone who has wronged us in any way. Although I say these words every day in my prayers, their meaning only then reached me—my sins will not be forgiven if I do not forgive others sincerely and ultimately.

The Holy Mass was followed by blessings given by Fr. Peter, starting with the sick in wheelchairs. Father Peter approached everyone, blessed them with a crucifix with the relics of saints, and asked "Do you believe in Jesus? Do you believe that Jesus can heal you?" Tears of emotion started to flow down many faces when one wheelchair-bound woman, held up by Father's hand, made a few steps. The prayer of the gathered people became still more fervent, when it had turned out that Fr. Peter was praying for deliverance of two individuals with demonic possession, which lasted quite a long time.

I looked intently at what was going on by the altar while standing in the chorus gallery of the church. Crowds of people were moving up for the blessing and time after time somebody fell down softly, held by catchers, onto the church floor, and experienced the Resting in the Holy Spirit. From afar, it looked as if they were fainting and it seemed a little shocking.

Some time later, I, too, approached the altar with a trembling heart.

I could not decide about my intention for which to receive the blessing. Of course, I have various health problems and spiritual dilemmas, but the problems of people close to me are also very painful.

I stood up not far from the Cross situated next to the altar, and I could not take my eyes off of it. I thought "God, You know my littleness, but if only You wish to come to me, then I am here, humbly waiting for You."

I do not remember the moment of the blessing. In the corner of my eye, I saw Fr. Peter coming my way. I felt two stronger beats of my heart and I fell down lightly. My earlier ailments disappeared: my back pain, my sore feet, the pressure in my breastbone—all that I linked to the excitement I felt at that time. I felt wonderful, so safe! I had a sensation of being wrapped in a warm soft blanket. I knew that there were other people close by me but kind of behind a wall. This was exactly like in the lyrics of the song: *In the light breath of air, You are coming to me, oh Lord.*

Words fail me to fully describe that moment of an all-embracing calm, joy, and trust; as well as gratitude and incredulity that it was I being in such bliss, for which, after all, I myself did nothing to deserve.

After a while, someone helped me sit down in a pew. Hot tears rolled down my cheeks but dried out quickly. My husband held me by the hand. Only then, still a little shocked and thrilled with the experience, could I take a close look at this unusual priest with great kindness and charisma, through whom God had given me proof of His Love, and showed that He cared for us and loved us.

How differently do I experience the Holy Mass nowadays. The words that I hear have gained a different and deeper meaning. My faith has grown stronger. When the time comes for receiving Holy Communion, a great feeling of joy and thankfulness fills me up.

I approach many matters and everyday duties with a greater involvement, calmness, and strength that I find within myself. I perceive more and more reasons to give thanks to God; often a smile appears on my face and I catch myself humming various religious songs or canons. I say almost every day the healing prayer written by Fr. Peter, and, now, I know for which intention to say it. Every single word of this prayer is dear to me.

Thank you, Fr. Peter, for your being so thoroughly a man of God and serving people with your gift received from God.

I am also grateful to our parish priest, Fr. Wojciech, for having invited Fr. Peter to our not so big parish.

We were able to see with our own eyes the Power of God and the effects of the working of the Holy Spirit then and there, so nearby; for some people, even in their hearts. We read about it in the Holy Scripture: *I will send down My Spirit on you,* or elsewhere, *the Apostles were healing the sick and casting out demons.*

So far I have received so much from God in my life; I have also experienced the touch of the Holy Spirit, and it is still transforming me. I pray to be able to give more of myself too, just straight from my heart, and not to stop giving thanks for those most beautiful experiences through which joy overfills me and my life has gained special brightness.

May God in His Kindness grant Fr. Peter Mary good health and blessing so that he may continue—for many years to come—helping needy people change and/or heal their wounded hearts and ailing bodies, because there are so many of them around us, after all.

Gratefully, Jolanta

I Encourage the Sick and Suffering to Say *The Miracle Prayer*

I went to the meeting with Fr. Peter because I was asked to be in a group leading the prayer at the meeting. So it was rather a kind of duty that caused me to come. I invited a few persons to the meeting, but they refused, excusing themselves for various chores and obligations. When I stood in the entrance door, I realized that I would not be able to get inside because of the crowd. I got there through the Sacristy to be near the altar.

I saw Fr. Peter at the concelebrated Mass presided over by Fr. Stanisław Kania. When the Holy Mass was over, I looked very skeptically at the people preparing us for receiving the blessing. Their mobility and boisterousness made me think that they were staging an American style show. Did those persons forget that they were at church? However, when I saw Fr. Peter and his humble profile, full of kindness and joy, my heart began to melt down. He disarmed me completely when I saw him kissing the hands of our Dean. I thought to myself: "What a great person you are, and full of humility." To receive his blessing, people had to get close to the steps at the foot of the altar. When Father approached me, he slightly faltered. I drew out my hands to hold him up, so that he would not fall down. Then Father gave me a penetrating look.

Having read the book about him, I realized with whom I really was meeting. What a devoted tool Fr. Peter was in the hand of the Lord God Himself! At the end of the old year, I thanked God for the gift of meeting with Father. The Lord, in the Advent season, had put in my way people who followed the path of holiness and at the same time desired for as many other people as possible to follow the same path.

The Miracle Prayer by Fr. Peter made a very strong impression on me. I thought to myself: "I thank You, Lord Jesus, and plead with You but I am not asking You for a miracle because my faith is little." I photocopied that prayer and I give it out. Whenever I meet with sick and suffering people, I talk to them about the meeting with Fr. Peter and encourage them to say *The Miracle Prayer*. Even if the Lord Jesus does not heal the body, He will surely fill our hearts with peace, joy, and the happiness of the imminent meeting with Him in eternity.

Halina

The Recession of a Long-term Disease

Jesus lives within the Church today and acts in the same way as 2000 years ago. He loves each one of us. He feels pity over our weaknesses and wishes to heal both our souls and our bodies. On the day of December 17, 2004, a common prayer vigil was organized at the St. Stanislaus Parish in Jasło, with a Holy Mass concelebrated by Fr. Peter Mary Rookey, OSM, followed by individual blessings of the gathered faithful.

As a parishioner, I participated in that event together with my husband in a group of persons who wished to obtain, by prayer, a spiritual grace for our families. I myself had suffered from an irregular peristalsis of the intestine for over 46 years and the medications did not help me. My entire body was impacted by the disorder. No physician could help me. Soon after my participation in Fr. Peter's service with *The Miracle Prayer*, I noticed that the disease had entirely receded. Further use of medications became unnecessary. I say *The Miracle Prayer* with faith, and the recovery of my strength as well as the efficiency of my system have become apparent. I shall add that it has been six weeks now since the time of the healing.

Thanks be to God.

A parishioner of St. Stanislaus Parish in Jasło

Czestochowa and, 8 Months Later, Kraków

It was in Czestochowa, where I saw Fr. Peter for the first time [April 2004]. It was cold, and everybody was wearing winter boots, while he was wearing sandals on his bare feet—moreover, he did not appear to be cold at all. Afterward, it turned out that Father had just returned from the Holy Land and, on his way back to the US, he briefly visited Poland and, of course, the Black Madonna. Undoubtedly, April in the Holy Land is pretty warm, but a pilgrim in sandals is rather a rare case to be seen in Poland during a cold April. I came to Jasna Góra with a group of Croatian pilgrims, and we were waiting for a prearranged Holy Mass in the Chapel of the Black Madonna. Thanks to that seemingly chance meeting, I got to know the wonderful priest, Fr. Peter. He and his entourage joined our group and participated in the Holy Mass in the Chapel of the Black Madonna.

Eight months later, Fr. Peter was in Krakow, where I was helping as an interpreter during the meetings for several days.

He is an exceptional person both as a man and as a priest. He lives the life of a true ascetic. He eats once a day and owns no material goods except for what is minimally necessary. I was deeply moved by the motto of Father, "A gift received becomes a good gift if it is forwarded to someone else." How many of us can live in true poverty?

Despite his age, he maintains his mental quickness and a splendid sense of humor. Even in time of disease, when most of us would simply become a burden on other people around us, he could still be joking. I was sincerely amused by a question asked of his assistant one morning. I think that Father himself did not feel at his best then, but—to avoid being questioned by others about his health—he turned it into a laugh right on the spot. Instead of his usual greeting to Jim, "How are you?" or "How do you do?"—he asked him, "Jim, are you going to live a little bit longer?" Even Jim, who had known Father for more than 20 years, appeared surprised by having been asked that unusual question at the start of another busy day.

I was greatly impressed by Father's readiness to serve other people. Despite an acute throat inflammation, an elevated temperature, and general weakness,

Father was serving the people by praying over them as he considered it to be his duty. Sometimes we took for granted (I would say—mercilessly) the fact that Father would not say 'No.' And Father, not having been informed earlier about a planned meeting, would go, no matter what.

He emanates unusual warmth. It seems that everybody feels good in his presence. It is hard to describe it, but it is as if he were sowing around himself the kindness of a man of God.

One more thing. During table-talks, Father's often slow talk showed his great fatigue. However, once he stood behind the altar, he changed completely. He stood up surely on his feet, his voice became pure, the words were articulated clearly, and—as Jim rightly noticed—even the wrinkles on Father's face smoothed. What a magnificent transformation! His God-given strength during his service at the altar could not be unnoticed even by people who see him for the first time.

Renata

His Greatest Gift for Others Is Prayer

Meeting with other people leaves traces in our lives. These traces, and their influences are great because as we constantly get in touch with others, they influence our own thinking about our lives. As the proverb says, "A person is known by the company he keeps."

I am a privileged person, because I have gotten in touch with many splendid people who have exerted significant influence on my life. Raised in compliance with the rule, "A guest in the house is God in the house," I experience that everyday.

Last year [April 2004], we had the privilege, as a family, to entertain Father Peter Rookey, OSM. It was a time of joy and learning to be with such an uncommon man. Observing Fr. Peter, we saw the words of the Bible seasoned into his ordinary life. Fr. Peter eats only one meal daily.Whenever he does not eat, he sits with others at the table and sips coffee with great human delight. He prays at every opportune moment. He holds his own body fit by doing physical exercises. He is always first to greet, is gallant toward women and friendly to animals. Meeting priests previously not known to him, he kneels and asks them for a blessing. He does not talk about his own gift of prayer, but he is a man conscious of the value of the priestly—Christly—blessing. Christ in the person of Fr. Peter is Christ who is intelligible by human measure—poor, joyful, focused on prayer, keenly listening, ready to give help, and, at the same time, showing that, in order to reach Him, it is necessary to try to do it through an internal discipline. If I were to define in one word what I saw in Father, I would say it is Humility.

Traveling with Fr. Peter is an adventure in solving difficulties. During his stay at the Jasna Góra Monastery, Fr. Peter had a desire to say a private Mass there. But there was a trifling problem—he did not have a document giving the permission that is necessary for every priest who wants to celebrate a Holy Mass in a place where he is unknown. After a moment of feverish pondering, we quite unexpectedly met a group from the region of Medjugorje who happened to be friends with Fr. Stanisław. The group was just about to attend a Holy Mass celebrated by their priest in front of the Black Madonna. Thanks to this coincidence, we were able to pray there, together with Fr. Peter concelebrating the Holy Mass.

Fr. Peter gave us a lot of presents. He arrived with a satchel filled with his documents and a small shopping bag with his personal things. He lavishly distributed his gifts, sometimes indispensable trinkets—like, for instance, when a rubber band was needed and could not be found in the whole big house, then he, most calmly, drew a rubber band out from his own bag. Whatever he gets, he soon delivers it to others. Just like it happened when our friend Barbara gave Fr. Peter a cap when they were in the Holy Land to keep him shaded from the sun. Father gave that cap to my husband. The true gift of Fr. Peter is prayer. Our household members, our family and friends, we all experienced the effects of his prayers: in our hearts—the relief of forgiveness, in our souls—a fuller trust in God, in our stamina—an ability to face life's hard challenges, and in our bodies—an effective resolve of health-related problems.

The greatest gift of Father's, while he briefly stayed in our house, was a Eucharist—with a gift of tears and a desire of offering our commonplaceness to God. In a post-Consecration prayer read then, I discovered a very moving, previously unknown to me text that reads, *Accept, oh Lord, all my freedom, accept my memory, mind, and all my will. Whatever I have, You gave it to me. All that I return to You and totally surrender to Your Will. Allow me only to love You and give me Your Grace, and I will be rich enough and thirst no more* [St. Ignatius].

That prayer became **my** prayer in a special way. One day, soon after the return of Fr. Peter to the States, I received a package from Barbara and, in it, there were the words of this prayer, my desired everyday prayer, beautifully framed. It was during the communal prayer during the Holy Mass said by Fr. Peter that I discovered what I needed in my daily life. So as not to let me lose this gift of insight while being perplexed with my duties, Barbara, a person fond of and capable of making gifts, through her present, gave me a chance to fulfill my prayerful passion.

It came as a great pleasure to me to be in the company of Fr. Peter: his Franciscan way of life, his smile, modesty, openness in meeting with another people or animals, his unostentatious and unassuming prayer that becomes a well-germinating grain in other people if only they are ready to accept it. Fr. Peter, understanding the busyness of the present times and the pursuance of duties, does not criticize; he only asks a question, "is there room/time for Jesus and Mary?"

I looked with concern at the great fatigue seen in Father during his healing ministry in Kraków. I was worried and shared the concern about Fr. Peter's state of health with the people who accompanied him during his visit to Poland. But when Fr. Peter was blessing the faithful—as my son noticed—his eyes were shining; they were joyful and not tired. On those days, I tried to call to my mind Fr. Stanisław's words, "you need to have trust in God."

I saw the grace of healing prayer received by the people leaving the church after the service—they were crying with the happiness of healed souls, and smiling to reflect internal joy and strength. I saw a deeply moved priest, whose prayers and blessings brought Resting in the Holy Spirit to quite a few people for the first time in his priestly life. And I saw the joyful experience of Resting in the Holy Spirit among those who had it for the first time ever.

Father Peter, like John Paul II, is fully devoted to Mary, an ascetic but enjoying his life, and focused on multiplying the talents he has received into a deposit for his Master. Father Peter, the loving priest, but—first of all—the priest living the proclamations of the Polish Pope fully.

So, yes, I really am a privileged person—I have met Father Peter Mary.

Dorota Ponikło

HE SERVES AND ACTS IN THE NAME OF JESUS

He can always be seen with a rosary in his hand, a white plastic rosary like those received at meetings with Fr. Jozo at Sirokij Brijeg, Bosnia & Herzegovina. The medium-size, broad-shouldered, handsome (at his age of 88 years) man in the black monk's frock, unceasingly uttering Hail Marys—such is a brief description of Fr. Peter Mary Rookey's *persona*. He visited Poland on December 10 through 21, 2004. The well-known charismatic, priest performing the ministry of prayer for the healing of the body and soul, but—first of all—he is a Servant of Mary by the name of the Order to which he belongs, as well as by his profound choice of serving "through Mary for the Glory of God."

While in Poland, Fr. Peter visited many places, starting in Bydgoszcz through Warszawa, Lowicz, Rzeszów, Jaslo, and Kraków. He was invited to hospitals and less official meetings. Every meeting with Father was accompanied by the masses, crowds, and flocks of the faithful reminiscent of the images in the Gospel, like, for instance, in Galilee, when the crowds were following Jesus, and *his heart was moved with pity for them, for they were like sheep without a shepherd* (Mk 6:34) and he healed them and set them free from demons. Also Fr. Peter—totally devoted to God as a burnt offering—did not stop blessing and—like the Holy Father John Paul II or Fr. Jozo Zovko—the more he gave himself up to the service of the people, the more he became invigorated, the more he looked as if he were "floating" among the crowds of faithful, when he was tirelessly blessing them. Everyone was astounded by the expression of his eyes and the lightness with which he moved (similarly to what I have once heard said about Fr. Daniel Ange at the Youth Festival in Medjugorje that "he not so much walks but more floats, carried by the Holy Spirit.")

And just as we read in the stories of the Gospel about the miracles performed by Our Lord Jesus, we also witnessed miracles worked through the ministry of Fr. Peter. This is nothing new or strange for those who believe in Jesus, because He Himself had announced: *whoever believes in me will do the works that I do, and will do greater ones than these* (Jn 14:12). The most significant example of that was the deliverance of a demon-possessed young woman who bore her personal testimony during Father's ministry in Krakow. Her possession was rooted in hatred. "Hatred can be an open door through which the devil can dominate a person" says Fr. Jozo Zovko.

Very often the reason for a lack of healing is lack of forgiveness that blocks the way for the grace; also the persistence in sin—we would like to have a healed body but without a healed spirit, so we continue to live in sin and suffer. Fr. Peter serves and acts in the name of Jesus. Even when he was unable to participate in services physically due to extreme fatigue, he was present at them in a spiritual way. The concerned faithful shared among themselves the news that "Father Peter got sick," but they failed to notice that Lord Jesus was healthy, and acted in His own Church.

Father Peter's exhaustion after numerous services to thousands of people called to my mind the sentence said by Saint John Vianney, the parish priest from Ars: "If the priest died of overwork or hardships sustained for the Glory of God and the saving of souls, it would not at all be a bad thing." I read that sentence for the first time at the Martha Robin retreat center, while on my way to meeting Fr. Peter in Warszawa. It appealed to me, and I began then to meditate on it, remembering the priests well-known to me who were devoted to the service of God with all their bodies and souls. During the prayer meetings with Fr. Peter, this sentence "was becoming flesh" within him—all the time indefatigable, seeing the poor souls in need, devoted until his "last breath." How much truth there is in this sentence of St. John Vianney—it seems that there is no life more beautiful for a priest than burning himself for the love of Jesus and neighbor. For a candle should burn, not smolder. Amen.

Ewa Jurasz

The Transformation of the Human Hearts

I met Fr. Peter twice, on the 16th and 19th of December 2004. I participated then as a seminarian in a Holy Mass and the charismatic prayer that he was leading. It was the first time I had a chance to take part in such a service and, in the beginning, I was a little bit lost and disoriented. But that feeling vanished quickly.

I want to say that during those days, what happened then, what God did for me and for other people, was something marvelous. I am not only talking about this, so to speak, on the outward side of the reality that can stir some sensation (because we cannot be witnesses even to Resting in the Holy Spirit frequently) but about the genuine transformation that occurred within the human hearts, about which I can speak as both a witness and a subject of such transformation.

The most important experience in the course of those days was what occurred to a young woman who was possessed by evil spirits. On Thursday, December 16, after the Holy Mass, the individual blessing of the gathered faithful began. When Fr. Peter approached that woman, she changed utterly. She started to fling, spit, and scream. Fortunately, having been forewarned earlier, we were prepared to face such a course of events. We rushed toward her. To show the scale of evil manifestation in her, it is necessary to say that she was held by seven stout, young men, because it was so hard to tame her. A longer than one-and-a-half-hour intercessional prayer over her ensued, delivered by all the priests attending the prayer service at the Pijarska Street, the seminarians, and the whole congregation still remaining at the church. Unfortunately, the Lord did not set her free then. We had to wait for that yet.

When I was returning home, I decided to pray fervently for her. I thought about it, and I realized in a somewhat different way what being a community was all about; in particular, the community of prayer. During my prayer, I felt as if I were near her, despite being tens of miles apart. However, the most important part was that, for the first time in my life, I was overfilled with great love—the Love of God toward me and her, as well as the brotherly love that brought me close to her. I really felt as if I were her blood-brother and I thought of her as my sister who needed help.

And, I gather, it is easy to surely imagine how I felt when I found out on Sunday that she was liberated, that the fiend had left her. I was simply walking on air. The joy that came over me was indescribable. I waited longingly for the moment when I would be able to see her and embrace her. I am glad that I could do it then. To me, that event is proof that the Lord continues to work through his apostles, that He still delivers us from evil spirits, not so much those which take control over us only physically, so to speak, as from those which rule over us in the spiritual domain—over making us sinners. And deliverance in that woman's case was and continues to be a sign of liberation from the evil destroying our souls.

The other phenomena that had an impact on me were those I observed in other people during the blessing, especially during their Resting in the Holy Spirit. I was a skeptic, but that changed when I saw people falling down like trees and pouring out torrents of tears. What struck me most was the expression on their faces when they were "asleep"—full of peace and happiness.

What still remains as the most interesting part is the person of Fr. Peter. Nowadays, there is an abundant "supply" of all manner of healers, bioenergy-therapists, and other witch curers. But Fr. Peter does not fit in with them. Why? Because he does not turn himself into a star; he does not put himself in the first place and, despite his age, he does not mind himself in his ministry.

In all those events I saw the presence of living Our Lord Jesus. They would not come to pass, unless for His Grace and the Spirit Whom He gave to us all. What He works through Fr. Peter is truthfully His own work and it is only He Who is to be credited for the miracles that I witnessed. And I thank Him for the abundant peace that He poured into me and which helped me take a different view of myself and the people around me as well as giving me strength in facing my hardships.

Michal Pękalski, SP

WHY DID YOU COME HERE?

My meeting with Fr. Peter came unexpectedly since I had learned about the meeting at the last moment. However, I realized immediately that I had to be there. I was pulled there by some great force. I was not scared of the crowds of people mingling in front of the Piarist Fathers Church—I was getting convinced more and more that I had to be there, because I wanted to be there. And no one and nothing could have discouraged me from being there, even though my husband was terrified at the sight of the crowd and wanted to give up.

I attended a Holy Mass in the church crypt, since it was impossible to enter the church. However, being in the crypt, I could feel the spirit of Fr. Peter perfectly well. I clearly saw the altar on the screen, but it was not the view that was all-important; it was the words—especially those said by Fr. Stanisław. What mostly appealed to me was his question: "Why did you come here?" Internally, I was calm and joyous, because it was only in this state that I could stay focused and contemplative, without forcing it upon myself, as I usually have trouble with focusing and concentrating. My body was fully relaxed despite standing on my feet throughout the long service. When the Holy Mass was over, I was standing in a line for 5 hours to get inside the church and receive a blessing from Fr. Peter. I looked at my husband, expecting to find him tired and bored; instead, I saw him smiling. The closer I was getting to Fr. Peter, the greater was the fear and anxiety I felt. Just before the grand moment, my body became numb. And, after that, I felt like I was reborn and had an incredible upsurge of energy. I remember that, when I came home. I was not able to fall asleep for a long time, because I was not tired at all, neither mentally nor physically. It was a happy day.

Agata

The Reality of the Presence of God and the Reality of the Presence of Satan

Not much time has passed since I had the opportunity to meet Fr. Peter Mary Rookey. That event, however, has entered deeply into my memory and my heart. Never before had I had an opportunity to attend a meeting with a man of special God-given gifts. Therefore, I wanted very much to experience that meeting with Fr. Peter, especially after hearing the testimonies of my fellow brothers from our other communities, in which Fr. Peter had already met with the faithful. Both the Thursday and Sunday Eucharists and the prayers were special times, replete with the Graces of God. The living and fervent prayers of the faithful gathered in the church, the view of the people experiencing the gift of Resting in the Holy Spirit, the fervent communal request to God for the deliverance from the devil, and the charismatic figure of Fr. Peter—all that made the experience of the real presence of God and His acts almost tangible.

The immediate contact with the person under the influence of Satan—her irate reactions and hatred toward the Holy Sacrament, the Holy Water, and the person of Fr. Peter—was an even stronger indication that Satan does exist, that the fight for human souls is really going on, that sin is not an insignificant matter, but also that the power and might of Jesus is greater and that it is He Who has won the battle. The person of Fr. Peter and the events that I witnessed also made me realize more deeply that the demons really fear and hate the priest but, as long as he remains faithful to Christ, he receives from Him a powerful authority.

This special time of Grace could be experienced by so many persons thanks to the presence of Fr. Peter in Kraków. I perfectly remember the moment when we were waiting somewhat impatiently for the coming of Father to the Sacristy as, by then, it was time to begin the Holy Mass. Nonetheless, as we found out, Fr. Peter, per Fr. Stanislaw's request, stopped once more on his way and entered a clubroom to bless children who spent their time on activities there, as well as their parents and educators. At last, there came the moment when Fr. Peter entered the Sacristy. From the first moment of His presence among the gathered people, I was fascinated by His great humility, simplicity, and enormous kindness toward the other man. This was especially visible on Sunday, when—exhausted by his illness and many hours' service—he was suffering all his ailments with huge sacrifice and meekness, many times staggering outright on his fatigued limbs, only to be able to bless the next person expecting to receive his spiritual support. It was clearly evident that this venerable old man, full of humility and meekness, as well as filled up with God's power at the same time, glowed with an immense love for every person standing up before him, as the person most important for him at the given moment.

As a Piarist priest and monk, I would like further to underline two attitudes of Fr. Peter that penetrated my heart particularly strongly:

1. His attitude toward priests. It was the priests with whom Fr. Peter always started his blessing and then he hugged each one of them, heart to heart, with his great paternal love. Certainly, in moments like those, his heart was beating with the burning desire that all priests have who are anxious about their personal holiness in helping Christ to draw human souls out of the enslavement by Satan and sin and lead them all to God.
2. His attitude toward children. As a Piarist [Order of the Pious Schools, in short Piarists], I was very moved when I saw Fr. Peter blessing a small child, and then take the child's little hand and kiss it. He taught us to see God in the other person, especially in the defenseless child.

May God be adored for all the goodness that He does through the people who wish to fulfill His Will in their own lives.

Fr. Józef M., SP

ALL DAY LONG AS IF IN THE ARMS OF GOD

When I found out that Fr. Peter, a charismatic who has received the gift of healing from God, would come to us, I was rather unmoved. And when I found out, on top of all things, that he had something in common with Medjugorje, I became closed, straight off to everything that had to do with that meeting—under no circumstances was I planning to go to it. However, seeing the need for help in organizing the meeting, I willy-nilly admitted that I would join.

My skepticism was gone in a blink of an eye as soon as I was standing on Pijarska Street (ha! ha!, so much that I was there all day long to attend each Eucharist!). At the beginning, I did not know what it was all about, but I felt that God was putting in place everything within me; efficiently getting to the bottom of my inner chaos and indifference. That peacefulness of my heart and the great prayer flowing out of me were inconceivable for me. All day long, I was as if in the arms of God—so I felt that I did not want to go back from there and, it was only I began to feel my strength dropping, I thought—enough was enough. **Something** forced me to stay, and gave me the strength needed. I know that it was the working of God. Fr. Peter, by putting down his feet on Pijarska Street, gave me the Grace of conversion and fervent prayer. Now I am involved in the New Evangelization Movement, a spiritual renewal fellowship. The experience of faith that I carried out of that meeting with God through Fr. Peter poured into my heart the hope and certainty that as long as God is with us whoever can be against us? Glory be to God for what He did for me then. Thank you Fr. Peter, the tool in the hands of God. I keep you in my prayers.

Michal Strojnowski, SchP

DOES SOMEONE FROM AMERICA REALLY HAVE TO COME?

I am one of those who waited for the arrival of Fr. Peter in Poland without any special enthusiasm. Granted, I read articles about him published in *Znak Pokoju* (*The Sign of Peace*) magazine, I held in my hand the book by the Irish author titled *Man of Miracles* translated into Polish, but I feared an atmosphere of sensation and that Father's ministry would be treated as magic. I have been a member of the Renewal in the Holy Spirit Fellowship for many years, and I saw with my own eyes wonderful cures many times. I also know that it is always the working of God, not man. Anyway, Jesus Himself promised that *These signs will accompany those who believe: (. . .) they will lay hands on the sick, and they will recover* (Mk 16:17-18). So, I thought: does someone from America really have to come so we can experience God's working?" Nevertheless, I saw the growing interest in Poland as I received a massive number of telephone calls with questions regarding the details about Fr. Peter's visit.

On the day of his arrival in Kraków, I found out that I was invited to a private meeting with Father arranged for persons associated with the Piarist Fathers' cloister. I thought that I would avoid getting into a crowd that way and, of course, I went there. It was a very short meeting, perhaps 10 minutes, but the immediate contact with the priest from Chicago was very positive: I saw a fair, smiling, elderly man beaming with kindness, and not devoid of a sense of humor, who could pray among the crowd, and encourage us to worship God. Modest, commonplace, straightforward—nothing of a self-called "healer," as I was afraid to find him to be. And, afterward, there was a Holy Mass, so fervently concelebrated by Father! And the adoration of Our Lord Jesus. And the people—elderly, wheelchair-bound or on crutches, perhaps even without any clear signs of being crippled or ill, but with hope and expectation shown on their faces. Some of them had waited for many hours in the cold until they could enter the church. I became ashamed of having gotten inside the church so easily through the Sacristy. However, when people began to advance, I retreated to make room for the sick, and I did not stay there until the end.

The echo of what had passed at the church began to reach me as early as the next day. I heard about people getting up from their wheelchairs and about some demon-possessed woman over whom a very long prayer had been said with little effect—it seemed. That happened on Thursday. On Sunday again, in the evening, I came running for a Holy Mass and, there, I saw a miracle happen before my very eyes: the woman who had been demon-possessed 2 days earlier was giving her testimony about her liberation and thanking Fr. Peter and everybody who had been praying for her! And her spiritual director confirmed in writing the miracle of her liberation. Fr. Peter himself was not present at that Sunday Holy Mass. He got sick after so many days of serving others. But Jesus directs everything. The absence of Father forced other priests and monks to administer the intercessional prayer for the faithful. And perhaps never until then had they done that, ever since the time of their first ordination Masses. But here they were laying hands on the sick and giving them the blessing. And the sick were healed—be it in the body or soul, which is known only to God since He acts in His way, treating everyone on an individual basis.

And this is exactly what I consider a Miracle: the reinvigoration of faith and love within the priests and their taking up the ministry of healing that is needed so much. I believe that this miracle will last and be expanded in our country, especially in the priests and the persons consecrated by the power of the Holy Spirit to go to the people in need. I see it happening already in some places; if some people do not believe it, let them come to the Piarists' Church in Kraków on every 16th and 25th day of the month at 6:00 PM and see it by themselves—Jesus lives and acts!

Anna Maria

The Holy Spirit in Action

Monday, December 13, 2004, at the Siekierki Sanctuary of Our Lady the Educatrix of the Youth, crowds of people converge on the sanctuary, tens of cars and motor coaches—such is the picture I see when I remember that day, the day which Our Good God planned to intersect my life path with that of the dear Fr. Peter Rookey for the first time.

When I entered the church, pushing through the crowd of the faithful, I found a place far and high on the balcony and, in anticipation of the commencement of the Eucharist, I began to meditate over how it had come about that I had come just to that place.

Information about that meeting had been reaching me for a month by then, but, being aware that Jesus lives among us, I did not feel the need to go to such a meeting. However, the Lord had planned everything otherwise. A variety of ups and downs in my family had caused me to seek advice in Jesus in the Sacrament of Confession. However, one of the Dominican Fathers, who is my spiritual supporter, had suggested that I needed some prayer for a deep internal healing, that somewhere within me there had been something resident since immemorial time, something that called for healing but was concealed from my eyes.

When the Holy Mass started, I felt the huge power of prayer within my soul. Despite the crowd around me, I felt like I was all alone with Jesus. It was just then that the Lord let me recognize in my heart that He was rendering me capable of fulfilling His Will, and that He was pouring into my heart immense Love for my fellow brothers and sisters. I took this to be a healing act of God, as a gift that I received in response to my many-year-long requests for the Grace of healing the internal wounds caused by people close to me.

I did not know what was happening, I do not remember the points of Fr. Peter's sermon, either. I was filled up by the Spirit of Peace and Love. After quite a long time, when I wanted to join the communal prayer, I sensed something odd happening, some restlessness and apparent irritation in the air. In addition, just after getting that feeling, I heard a horrible scream, the kind of scream with which I was familiar by then, and I felt perfectly clear what it was about. I started to pray, first in tongues; then I began saying the Rosary.

I did not feel the need to get any nearer to it. By then, I had previously helped on several occasions with deliverance prayers, the exorcist prayers; I even had participated in exorcisms and had already experienced the power of humble and fervent prayer in such situations.

At about 9:30 PM, the church began to empty and I went down to receive the blessing from God through the hands of Fr. Peter. When my turn came, I did not look at Fr. Peter; I completely surrendered myself to the work of the Holy Spirit. Fr. Peter went away from me and had already blessed the next person when, all of a sudden, he returned to me and whispered a *Thank you* into my ear. It paralyzed me.

When I sat down in the pew to pray, one thought pervaded me: what did he thank me for? It was I who should have thanked Him. I did not understand what he meant.

Then the Lord stirred a desire in my heart to ask Father for an individual prayer. Unfortunately, it turned out that Father had gone. Then Barbara crossed my way. We had not met before and I did not know that she was the one who had arrived there with Fr. Peter. Barbara told me that, on the next day, Father would be in Lowicz and that, if I wanted, I could go there. I was reluctant to go to Lowicz. I started to withdraw from that meeting. I thought that, after all, God will do what He wants right here in Warszawa, that I do not need to go such a long way only to be in a big crowd again and that, anyway, the trip would also cost me money.

When the next morning came, I found myself again at Siekierki, but for a limited time. It was not possible for me to meet with Fr. Peter and ask for a private conversation with him. Barbara advised me again with great confidence and resolve that I should go to Lowicz. In a split second, I made up my mind; I will go there. At the same moment, I saw Jim.

I offered to take a joint trip with several persons, but, in the end, nobody was able to go there with me. I did not realize then that I would be involved in a great service to God at the side of His beloved son, Fr. Peter; that my stay there would be extended from 2 hours to over a week; and that God would take me from Lowicz through Rzeszów and Jaslo to Kraków.

*   *   *

In my memory, I recall the moment of the meeting. First, Fr. Stanislaw Kania got out of the car, then Barbara, Jim and, finally, Fr. Peter. I remember his smile, the smile from which one can read, 'good to see you, I was expecting you.'

Out in Lowicz, there were many signs indicating the Lord was expecting something of me. Things like Fr. Peter's smile; Barbara seeing two beds in her room and saying that the extra one was probably meant for me; or my finding a certain amount of money covering evenly the sum spent on purchasing the gas on the way to Lowicz. However, when Fr. Stanislaw asked me to provide further service during a Mass with Fr. Peter, my first answer was "No."

I remember the Holy Mass in Lowicz. There I felt the presence of the Spirit of Unity. There were a great many people but everything went smoothly. I still can see Fr. Peter walking from brother to brother, from sister to sister and pleading for God-given Graces when laying his hands on the people's heads. I also remember the way Satan began to manifest himself in the body of a young woman held in my arms. It was a hard case, very hard, indeed.

I have the image of all this in my mind. Through the mouth of that young woman, the devil is speaking blasphemies against God. So, we begin the prayer for her liberation. He spits at Jesus in the Holy Sacrament. He spits at Fr. Peter calling him names and insulting him. He curses in Polish, English, and Latin. He tries to play his tricks on the other priests. He changes his voice, tries to be chummy, sometimes . . . amorous.

Soon after that, the demon reveals itself in the body of a mentally disturbed teenage boy. His neurological condition only adds to the problem. Three persons show signs of being seized by the devil on that day. I also remember the intense aggression of those persons when they are approached by Fr. Peter. And I remember his great love for them throughout the service. Father's great humility and love catch my eye. He prays patiently, lying prostrate before Jesus. He asks Jesus to show His Mercy and deliver those persons from the evil spirit. He is doing it under insults and threats thrown in his face.

The prayers of that day end late, at about midnight. I am tired and decide to stay overnight. It is during supper when Fr. Stanislaw proposes that I go on with Fr. Peter's group the next day to Rzeszow. I am completely unprepared for an extended trip, and I do not want to go, but the Lord asks me in my heart if I love him? . . . Yes, my Lord.

*   *   *

We go to Rzeszów. The travel is hard and takes about 6 hours. We are driving up the street leading to the church and are having trouble with getting there. There are crowds and crowds of people everywhere. We are tired, but Fr. Peter is humbly going toward the church. He is going to those who have been waiting for him, waiting for almost 4 hours now. At this moment, I notice that Fr. Peter is not eating anything. Barbara confirms that Father eats only once a day, after the Eucharist. The Lord reminds me that . . . *this kind of spirit does not come out except by prayer and fasting.* And, in His infallibility, He knows when to remind me of that fact.

Fr. Stanislaw asks me to instruct the people responsible for keeping order, assisting with the liturgical service, and the novices before the start of the Holy

Mass regarding the service schedule; he especially asks that I instruct them about what kind of surprises to expect. I ask them to prepare the monstrance, plastic mugs, towels, and . . . Holy Water, lots of it, to the surprise of the brother sacristan. The surprise and disbelief of these young men show on their faces when I try to describe the possible situations. My full-fledged service in Fr. Peter's team is now set off.

The team is made up of five persons: Fr. Peter, Fr. Stanislaw, Jim, Barbara, and I.

During the Eucharist, I do experience a personal meeting with my Lord . . . During the Holy Mass, the Lord inspires me so that the three of us would receive the Holy Communion under two species. I tell Fr. Stanislaw about it; he reacts immediately. This Holy Mass is special for me; I receive many graces that prepare me for the healing service, for service in the name of Jesus continuously living among us.

Of that evening, I remember that there were many handicapped persons. Fr. Peter approached those persons in the first instance—he blessed, hugged, and smiled at every one of them. He carried Love to them, the Love of the Good God. I do not remember if there were any physical healings among those persons; at that time, I had to see about rather down-to-earth matters.

In one moment, the order-keeping service lose control over their duty; a terrible commotion and confusion erupt. Then a thought comes to me that I will need to buckle up for a "confrontation" likely to come up soon.

In the same moment, Fr. Peter asks for the exposition of the Lord Jesus and a common, fervent prayer.

A few minutes later, I see a young boy lying on the floor. At first look, it seems to be as if he were resting in the Holy Spirit. But his head is under a bench, and it is dangerous, because when he wakes up from resting, he could injure himself unconsciously. I start to pull him out from under the bench, and then I sense his body begin to tremble. At first, the trembling is slight; I begin to pray in tongues, asking the Holy Ghost to come over him entirely and, then, there comes an attack of terrible aggression. I try to block him with all the weight of my body. I see the shock in people around me, the expression in the eyes of a doctor who wants to give first aid, and then I see his bafflement. Love is invincible, however. The fear passes quickly.

Men try to transfer this youth hurriedly to the Presbytery, before the Face of the One Who Is Omnipotent.

In the corner of my eye, I see Fr. Peter interrupt his blessing of the faithful and walk toward the Presbytery. My attention concentrates, however, on a very young girl laying nearby. She is, seemingly, also resting in the Holy Spirit. She is weeping.

Like always, the Holy Ghost comes whenever and however He wants. Often it is manifested by crying; but that girl's crying is different. I kneel down by her and start to pray; her body begins to writhe. Her girlfriend standing by her says that the three of them came to this Mass—the third was the boy over whom Fr. Peter is now bending. The girl is also carried over to face Jesus Christ's Power.

In unison with the priests, we begin to pray over the two possessed youngsters. Satan steps up his aggression. The mouths of those youngsters spew out inhuman snarls, howling, roars, and blasphemies. Blasphemies against God, in particular. Each one of them is held by a few strong men. We say prayers for their liberation and exorcism prayers.

Fr. Peter is praying composedly; he is radiating Peace and Love. He is all in Christ and Christ in him, which can not only be sensed but also seen.

Suddenly there is silence, as the demon gives up on those youngsters. Father returns to his own "work," ie, blessing the faithful. Despite his fatigue and advanced age, he walks through the church unrelentingly, blessing everyone. He anoints every head, lays his hands on, and pleads with the Good Father for everyone. There will be many such passes and turns today for hours and hours. I hear it again in my heart: *this kind of spirit does not come out except by prayer and fasting.*

I look at the whole church. I see how much the Lord is doing here. I can feel the huge power of the communal prayer delivered in One Spirit. All the hearts at the church are calling out, "Veni Sancte Spiritus, Veni Sancte Spiritus, Veni Sancte . . ." Some people rest in the Holy Spirit, others receive the Gift of Peace and Joy, still others the Gift of Tears, some people leave like they came in but—after a while—it turns out that they, too, have not been overlooked in the generosity of Our Redeemer. And Fr. Peter, in his humility and Love, is passing from the left to the right . . .

Of that evening, one image stays stored deeply in my memory. At a certain moment, I hear a loud sob; I look toward the spot from where it is coming from, and I see a young man sobbing in the arms of Fr. Peter. He looks like a little boy sinking in his daddy's arms. The view is poignant and so inexpressibly beautiful. Father looks into my eyes; I approach them both. I hug that brother of mine and begin to worship the Good God within him for the Graces granted. And, just in that moment, this man begins to reveal all his weaknesses. His entire body expresses the pain caused by those weaknesses. The Lord allowed me to learn that, in that moment, He was coming to his own son with all His Graces through the Sacrament of Repentance and Reconciliation. Before my very eyes, the Holy Confession is taking place. I sense Jesus silencing the storm in his heart time after time and see the changing face of this man.

Much later, our eyes cross, when he is to receive Holy Communion. His happy face beams, and his eyes speak with joy about the Power and Omnipotence of Jesus Christ, about the great and infinite Love that He has for us. I trust God healed his own son then and gave him the power to persevere.

The prayers over the possessed persons last until late, and Father continues for a long period to cast out the demons. From time to time, I see his body weakening, but as soon as he takes the Monstrance again into his hands, his eyes start to burn and the Spirit begins to act in the unimposing and fatigued body of this humble Servant of Mary.

*   *   *

After supper, despite being tired, Father blesses the gathered priests and novices once more before he leaves to sleep.

Next day, we leave for Kraków after a short night sleep. We plan on having a Holy Mass, followed by Fr. Peter's blessing. Right then, I have the pleasure to give a ride to Fr. Peter in my car and have the joy of being with him away from the crowds, in peace and quiet. I have a chance to take a closer look at this uncommon, modest, and meek man. I can not only see how close he is to Jesus and Mary but I also can feel it. And I realize this soon after leaving the church's gate behind. When we were leaving Rzeszów, everybody was telling me how to get to Kraków and the Piarists' Church there. I even received a sketchy drawing of the route; no one, however, explained how to get out of Rzeszów itself. So, I began to pray to the Holy Spirit to give me an inspiration and to Mary to be my guide. Literally, a moment later, as we drive up to a roundabout without any road sign, Fr. Peter turns to us saying: "Look, that light over there is not green, it's blue" and, after a while, he adds: "We're being guided by Mary."

It is a great experience for us when, taking the successive roundabouts and intersections one by one after switching into the right lanes, it turns out that we are going in the right direction each time.

At the beginning of our ride, Fr. Peter is invigorated, joyful, and interested in the sights of Rzeszów but, on leaving the city behind, he draws out his rosary and starts to pray. I see him in the rear mirror; I see how stressful for him the ride is and how much he suffers in silence. It is hard for him to find a comfortable position, his leg is getting numb and he is cold. I realize that, after all, he is 88 years old and he could actually have stayed at his home, to relax, read, or walk. Yet he serves for many hours on end. He serves his brothers and sisters. He bears witness to the Living God about His Love for us.

The trip itself all the way from Chicago is a reason why even young people have to accommodate and acclimatize, whereas he comes ready to share the Goodness that he has received from Jesus Christ.

The road is jammed up from dense traffic at the peak hours in Kraków. This extends the time of our driving to 4 hours. It appears to me, from time to time, that Father is asleep, but whenever I look at him, he opens up his eyes and smiles at me. I guess Christ smiles at us that way whenever He looks at us.

We get onto the Pijarska Street with difficulty; as a matter of fact, we do it thanks to the policemen who enable us to drive up to the church. (We did not know that the throng was made by the people waiting for the Holy Mass, in which we were about to participate.) We take a brief moment of rest after the tiring trip. I get down to the Sacristy to meet with the order-keeping service. I meet young men there, their faces showing concern, uncertainty, maybe even some fear. They are seminarians. They have heard what was going on in Rzeszów.

I try to explain to all of them the plan of today's meeting. I ask them to bring in plastic cups, towels, Holy Water . . . I learn that the Mass will be attended by the woman "liberated" back in Lowicz. We are in for a long evening. Father Peter appears a short time later, not resting anymore, fasting, and I remind myself of the words: *this kind of spirit . . .*

*   *   *

It seemed to me that the evening of that day would never come to an end. Fr. Peter was blessing people for several hours. He anointed everyone with oil, laid his hands on their heads, hugged, and smiled at them. Many people rested in the Holy Spirit, many continued to give longer thanks for the Graces received from God. When the last person went away back from the altar, Father turned back toward the Presbytery and, then, a real battle between good and evil broke out. Fr. Peter fulfilled persistently the task that Jesus had left for His Apostles when giving them the power over the unclean spirits.

That evening, Fr. Peter was very exhausted, but his weariness was not conspicuous to everybody. I think, actually, I am certain this weariness reflected the struggle from Fr. Peter's fighting with the devil for the soul of that young woman. How great that struggle was can be attested by the fact that, on the next day, Father's body was very feeble, his system weakened, and he got a fever. However, this friar, man of deep faith and humility, was not taking any rest. In total submission to the Will of God, he took up again the hardships of his pilgrimage. This time, he was on his way to serve his brothers and sisters in yet another city, in Jaslo. To serve their faithful inhabitants with his love and humility.

*   *   *

I remember that Mass, and I see before my eyes the image of a tired and stooping man.

Now, as I recollect all that, I see the vast and incomprehensible Love of God for His children, His care to provide for them everything they need and nothing more than they can carry. This Holy Mass was dominated by imperturbable peace, the blessing went on briskly, despite quite a large number of people. Everything lasted for about 2 to 2.5 hours . . . *Your Father knows what you need . . .* God knew that His son needed some easier work.

That led us to Sunday. The day awaited by many people.

Fr. Peter had been weakened since Thursday; he was in fever and spoke with a hoarse voice. We had no idea if he would be able at all to go down to the church, considering his condition. After a discussion with Jim, a decision was made that Father would only be giving a blessing.

Jim is a member of the International Compassion Ministry and of the Secular Servites and has worked for Father for 20 years in his ministry. He is a cheerful man, humbly keeping aside, ready to take up many sacrifices. Like Fr. Peter, Jim is quiet, modest, and patient during all hardships.

At the morning Holy Mass, Father was blessing everyone individually. At the second Holy Mass, there were so many people that a decision was made to go around the church in a procession with the Most Holy Sacrament. The seminarians made up a little cordon to make it easier for us to pass through the church. Father followed the priest who carried the Monstrance, giving his blessing; some people were melting down falling into Resting in the Holy Spirit as the procession was passing by. When I rerun this image in my mind, I see Jesus walking among his people and they all . . . *begged him that they might touch only the tassel on his cloak . . .*

Of that Mass, I particularly remember one woman who started to moan terribly after being blessed by Fr. Peter. Her body was in spasms from crying. Passing by her, I asked for someone to hug her as I had a feeling that a miracle of internal healing was happening in her. I myself had the duty to follow Fr. Peter, but I could not leave that sister in a state like that. It was the Love that I received from Jesus that made me return to her. So we were both standing there despite the crowd pressing against us. She cuddled in my arms, all in tears; and I was praying for her with all my might asking God for the Grace of comfort and to heal her. I felt that her soul was tearing apart in despair. I did not know how long we were standing like that, but I felt the Holy Spirit come over her with His comfort, healing, and forgiveness. On leaving her, I saw a faint smile appear on her face.

That day God did a lot in that place. I remember one of the altar boys resting in the Holy Spirit, lying with his eyes wide open, tears the size of peas flowing down his cheeks; and the expression on his face was as if he were walking in Heaven. Later on, he was sitting in a pew crying and laughing interchangeably.

I remember a cynical young man from the Maltese Aid service who, while standing in line for a blessing, was making fun of the people resting in the Holy Spirit. Father Peter did not quite touch his head and he was now lying stretched out on the floor. He, too, did not return to his assigned duty soon. In solitude, he was re-living for a while his encounter with God.

I wish to share yet another joyful, actually funny, experience. When Fr. Peter was relaxing in between the morning blessings, I was passing repeatedly between the Sacristy and the room in which he was resting.

At one of the turns in the hallway, I met a 4- or maybe 5-year-old girl with Down syndrome. She had beautiful, untied blond hair. When I stopped by her and asked what her name was, she stretched out her arms toward me, wrapped them around my neck and said "Julia." I asked her mom to stay there with her daughter, because I wanted to introduce her to Father. When finally Father came up to her, she touched his beard saying, "Gee whiz, this is Saint Nicolas." God *did* give us some real cheer.

The next Mass, celebrated in the afternoon, was delayed and ended shortly before the evening Mass. Fr. Peter concelebrated it and blessed the people in person. He refused to give out a general blessing since God had ordered him to bless the faithful and give out the sacramentals individually to each person present. I do not know whether there were 4000 or 5000 heads that he touched during that service, but the ministry seemed to me to last without end.

We were also given the great joy of seeing the Might of the Omnipotent God confirmed. The woman over whom we were praying back in Lowicz and Kraków came and gave her public testimony of being delivered from the power of the devil.

Physically, it was a hard job to do. Spending several hours in the car, then standing on one's feet in the crowd for several hours each time; but what a joy filled up my heart, what Peace overcame my soul, and what Love I carried in me, that I am unable to describe.

I slept 4 hours a day, but I did not need to sleep. God regenerated my strength by letting me be with Him; all I needed was a few minutes of Resting in the Holy Spirit to confess with all my heart . . . *here I am, send me* . . .

On the eve of his departure, Father concelebrated a Holy Mass at the Chapel in the Monastery of the Sisters of Our Lady Mother of Mercy at Łagiewniki. It was celebrated for the intention of the girls under the care of the sisters. There, too, the Lord did not spare his Graces on us.

Finally, the day of my friends' departure arrived. My heart was overcome by the feeling of sadness. We were together one whole week for almost all of the time. We gathered with Jim, Barbara, Fr. Stanisław and Fr. Tomasz, the rector of the church at Pijarska Street, at about 8:00 AM. We were getting ready for the moment of saying "Good-bye" and parting with each other, when Fr. Peter came in and up to me to say "Hello" as he used to say every morning. This time he said "I dismiss you from your job, now you can go home." At that moment, I remembered his "Thank you" said to me in Warszawa and that mysterious but meaningful smile in Lowicz. Now I am sure that he had to know in the first second of our meeting that God had decided to show me His Magnitude, Kindness, Generosity, Care and, above all, to show me that . . . *He loved his own in the world and he loved them to the end* . . .

*　　*　　*

Just minutes before Father's departure for the airport, a man came up and gave Fr. Peter a beautiful white stole as a token of his gratitude and thanks. He said that he had a good reason to be thankful, because he had lost his will of life completely due to his illness (cancer). Last Thursday, he attended the Holy Mass at the Piarists' Church in Kraków. During the blessing, he felt a wave of heat going through him. He did not know if he had been healed from his illness then, but he had regained his will and joy of living.

I could see and feel all that thanks to the faithfulness of the humble servant, Fr. Peter Mary Rookey, the friar priest from the Order of the Servants of Mary in the USA.

Glory be to You, Jesus, for Your Love that You have for me, for the Holy Spirit Whom you send down on me. I thank you for every brother and sister whom I could serve in Your Name. For Fr. Stanisław who, I trust, was inspired by the Holy Spirit to invite me to the service, for Jim's smiling eyes, for Barbara's joy and sense of humor, for the hospitality of Fr. Tomasz, and other Fathers and Parish Priests. But most of all, I would like to thank My Lord for Fr. Peter. For his being Your witness, for his having accepted Your Word, and, finally, for bringing to us Hope, the Hope that You live and are here with us through all the days until the end of the world.

I shall never forget that retreat for the rest of my life.

In the Spirit of Love and Peace,

Urszula Uljasz

Postludium

To Fr. Peter MARY Rookey

Nazarene
born for the USA
Padre Pio
assigned
to St. Bonfilius Priory

To look for visible
stigmata
or wounds
in you
would be in vain!

Hidden
deeply
in your heart
they bleed
heavily
inward
Barbara Wojtowicz

The power of the real healing comes only from God.

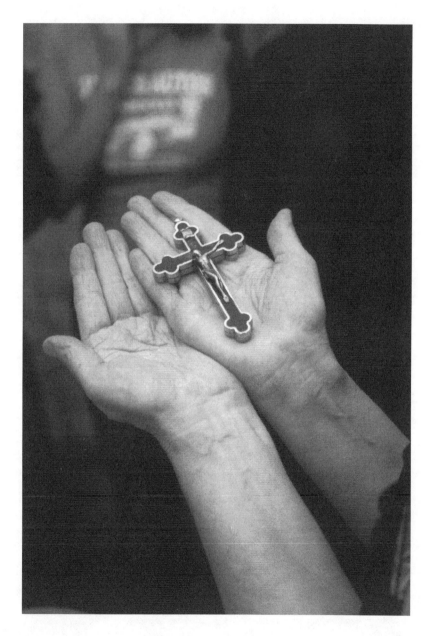

The precious crucifix (with relics of the Seven Founders of the Order of Servants of Mary and St. Juliana, St. Peregrine, and St. Philip Benizi) is used by Fr. Peter Mary to bless people. Holding it by a lay person is always meant as a great grace.